Enjoy!
Dad Dut

On Purpose

Stories from the Lives of Oregon
Nonprofit Leaders

On Purpose

Stories from the Lives of Oregon
Nonprofit Leaders

David Dickson

Copyright © 2020 by David Dickson

All rights reserved

Designed by Rose Dickson

Contents

Foreword	1
Introduction	7
I. Life Changing Events	15
The Fighter—Alberto Moreno	17
The Calling—Father Dick Berg	22
The Organizer—Marcy Westerling	27
The Point Guard—Tony Hopson, Sr.	32
The Outsider—Andrea Williams	38
II. Overcoming Barriers	47
The Mentor—Duncan Campbell	49
The Reformer—Paul Solomon	55
The Sister—Genny Nelson	62

The Storyteller—Trish Seiler	69
The Rebel—Michael Eichman	76
III. Collaboration	**83**
The Scientist—Dr Kent Thornburg	85
The Lightning Rod—Sam Skillern	91
The Elder—Terry Cross	98
The Dreamer—Mark Langseth	104
The Community Builder—Kelly Poe	109
IV. Giving Back	**117**
The Doctor—Dr Jill Ginsberg	119
The Counselor—Margaret Carter	125
The Coach—Bob Lieberman	130
The Foster Parent—Mary Collard	137
V. Advocacy	**145**
The Vista Volunteer—Rachel Bristol	147
The Justice Seeker—Ramon Ramirez	154
The Believer—Rita Sullivan	160
The Quiet Leader—Brenda Johnson	167
The Writer—Rich Wandschneider	174
VI. A Later Calling	**183**
The Tanzanian—Barry Childs	185
The Orchestrator—Sharon Morgan	191
The Environmental Entrepreneur—Brad Chalfant	198

The Teacher—Debbie Vought	206
The Black Pioneers—Willie Richardson and Gwen Carr	213
VII. New Approaches to Leadership	**225**
The Newcomer—Roberto Jimenez	227
The Salvage Entrepreneur—Terry McDonald	235
The Pragmatic Idealist—Swati Adarkar	242
The Traveling Teacher—Bill Rauch	246
Acknowledgements	**255**

Foreword

by Duncan Campbell

Five years ago, when David Dickson asked to interview me for his book on Oregon nonprofit leaders, I agreed with no hesitation. I figured that my story might encourage others to follow their passion to serve the community.

The story of my journey is chronicled in chapter two of this book. Growing up as a youth in inner-city Portland, I never had adult role models to show me the way out of a life of poverty. Through a combination of determination and good fortune, I was able to redirect the trajectory of my life, get an education, and found a business.

Ten years into a successful business career, it became clear to me that there was something missing in my life, a higher sense of purpose. In 1993 I began the process of selling my business and starting a new career, which led to the founding of

Friends of the Children in Portland and several other nonprofit organizations supporting youth. The inspiration to found this mentoring program for kids was the fact that I didn't have a mentor myself while growing up, and I didn't want another child to have the painful childhood I experienced.

Five years after he interviewed me, David Dickson shared with me a manuscript of his book. *On Purpose: Stories from the Lives of Oregon Nonprofit Leaders* exceeded my expectations. Through an impressive collection of stories told by the leaders themselves in an intimate interview format, Dickson is able to capture the lives of a widely diverse group of nonprofit leaders. The book focuses on the spark that grew into a powerful sense of purpose which led each of these leaders to pursue a career of helping others.

The stories are both easy to read and uplifting: the story of the misfiring gun that inspired Tony Hopson to found Self Enhancement Inc; Dr. Jill Ginsberg's story of answering a pastor's call to found the North by Northeast Community Health Center; the harrowing experiences in Italy as a young exchange student that led Marcy Westerling to establish The Rural Organizing Project; Paul Solomon's evolution from an incarcerated criminal to an advocate for ex-convicts transitioning back to society.

At the same time touching, poignant and meaningful, each story provides a different perspective. Together they form a rich mosaic of human experience. What unites them is the "fire in the belly" (to use the author's words) that inspired all 34 people to pursue their passion through nonprofit work.

Foreword

On Purpose is a must-read for anyone who is either seeking or already established in a nonprofit career. Based on my own experience founding and leading nonprofit organizations, it is not only the tools and strategies of successful nonprofit work that will determine success. More importantly, it is the intangible value of motivation and inspiration, derived from a clear sense of purpose. This book provides both. By understanding the deeply personal life stories of successful leaders, tomorrow's leaders will find their own unique pathways to success.

But the audience should not be limited to existing and aspiring nonprofit leaders or to the geographic confines of the state of Oregon. Anyone who wants to understand the inspiration behind a group of unsung heroes quietly changing lives in the nonprofit world should read this book.

On Purpose comes at a turning point for our country. There has never been a greater need to serve others and to come together as a community. We are a complex and often divided community, but it is what we have in common that makes us strong. By giving each of the 34 interviewees in this book the simple prompt, "Tell me about your life and what inspired you to do the work you do," David Dickson has given readers a glimpse into those elements of our common humanity that make nonprofit work a fundamental pillar of strength and unity in our increasingly diverse society.

Duncan Campbell
January, 2018

Foreword

Author's note: Duncan Campbell is the founder and Chairman Emeritus of Campbell Global, a timber investment firm. He holds a B.S. Degree and a Doctor of Jurisprudence Degree from the University of Oregon. He is the founder of four children's organizations, including the nationally known Friends of the Children. He is the author of "The Art of Being There," which tells his story leading to the founding of Friends of the Children in 1993 and the stories of the children and youth in the program. In 2009 he won the prestigious National Purpose Prize from Civic Ventures for his impact as a social entrepreneur and champion for children.

Introduction

Launching an Encore Career

In the spring of 2010 I was 60 years old and just two months away from my announced retirement. The prospect of unlimited free time was both enticing and daunting. As a child of the 60s, my career had been driven by John F. Kennedy's challenge, "Ask not what your country can do for you. Ask what you can do for your country."

I was ready to retire from higher education fundraising and marketing, which had been the focus of my work for 25 years. But there remained a passion in my soul which dated back to my early 20s, when I was a VISTA volunteer community organizer in some of the nation's poorest communities in eastern Oklahoma. That passion for bringing people and communities together around social justice and improving the quality of life never left me. I was also very fortunate that my community college and university employers had supported my pro bono strategic planning and development work with nonprofit organizations throughout my career in community service.

I knew intuitively that a retirement of leisure alone would not satisfy that very elemental need I had for a sense of purpose and contribution to the greater good. Envisioning an "encore career" in consulting for nonprofits, I put up my shingle and started to get the word out that I was available. But the thing that really captured my imagination was a project I took on to prepare me for my consulting work. I began interviewing successful nonprofit leaders, with the goal of discovering the best practices of those who were most successful in our community. It struck me that there were dozens of reference books on best practices in the private sector, most notably Tom Peters' *In Search of Excellence*. I found no similar reference library for the nonprofit sector. I determined that I would have to do the research myself.

The areas of nonprofit leadership that attracted me the most were strategic planning, developing nonprofit boards, building organizational culture, and inspiring staff to do great work—maybe a bit about fundraising too.

I started setting up hour-long interviews, beginning with a broad question, "What people and events in your life inspired you to get involved in nonprofit work?" Then I'd tackle each of the core areas of their work, from strategic planning to building organizational culture, in order to glean best practices. I explained my purpose to interviewees as capturing those best practices in order to share them with the next generation of nonprofit leaders.

A Change of Direction

Two things happened to me as I launched the interview process. First, I read Leslie Crutchfield and Heather Grant's book, *Forces for Good*, which focuses on case studies of successful nonprofits and six powerful themes that are common in their success. It is an outstanding book, which I would recommend to anyone who is involved in nonprofit work. It blew me out of the saddle! There was no way I was going to put together anything that would add significantly to the study of best practices that these two authors crafted.

The second thing that happened to me was even more jolting. It began with my first interviewee, Fr. Dick Berg, a tall Holy Cross Catholic educator and priest with a perpetual twinkle in his eye. We never even got to interview question two as we nibbled on Chinese buffet and talked about the people and events that had inspired Dick. Of particular interest to me was his experience meeting a homeless person just after he was assigned as pastor of Portland's St. Vincent de Paul Downtown Chapel. After a long career in higher education, this new role was a challenge for Dick. He credits this "street angel" with answering his prayer and inspiring him in his new assignment of urban healing.

As I continued doing interviews, a problem kept recurring. I was having a hard time keeping myself and my interviewees awake once I moved into questions about strategic planning, organizational culture, fundraising, and other nonprofit best practices. It seemed that all of them had read the same books or listened to the same experts. In fact it was my first question—about people and life events that influenced and inspired these leaders—that animated my subjects and captured my attention. A dozen interviews into the process, I finally accepted the reality of the situation: it was the life stories, not the best practices, which got my heart beating and energized my subjects. This would become the focus of my book.

Fire in the Belly

My interview questions were now limited to one—who were the people and what were the events that led to your career in nonprofit work? I was inspired by the answers I was given to this question. They reflected the "fire in the belly" which my now-deceased friend Frank Elardo talked about as the essential quality for a person who wants to make a difference in the community. A former high-tech executive who advocated for abused and forgotten young women to find purpose in life through education, Frank "got it". And he helped me get it. "Fire in the belly" can't be taught. It comes through life experience, through pain, through a deep connection with people. Career advancement and financial success rarely are the driving force. That fire arises from a deep, personal sense of purpose.

Thus, the initial interviews led me to discover **my** purpose—to tell the stories of the people who are making a difference in the life of our community—their origins, setbacks, discoveries, mentors, triumphs, and reflections on life and purpose. Several people suggested that I go outside Oregon and seek out leaders who have made a difference around the country and even internationally. I rejected that idea, because I wanted these stories to be about the communities where we live and work and play. I wanted to shine light on the people and events that typically occur in the shadows of our communities, events we may not see, but that bring people together, bring about change, and transform lives.

I still wanted to inspire the next generation of leaders with these stories—to give them role models and points of reference as they launch out to try to improve the quality of life around them. At the same time, I wanted our entire community to hear these stories, gleaned from over eighty interviews over an eight-year period. These stories have inspired me. My hope is that they will inspire many others to encourage and support these life changers in their work to make our communities better.

The Interviews

This book tells the stories of 34 Oregon nonprofit leaders. I interviewed over 80 people during a time span of eight years from 2010 to 2017. Many of the individuals featured in these stories have achieved notoriety, but others are virtually unknown outside of the communities and lives they have served.

In order to help the reader understand the work that these individuals have done, I have noted personal and organizational accomplishments. But the purpose of this book is not to highlight accomplishments; instead it is to tell the stories of what inspired them. The format of the book reflects this purpose. The interviews are presented in the present tense. Accomplishments are noted based on the time of the interview. I have added *Author's Notes* in two cases where the interviewee died subsequent to the interview, and included updated information in other cases where changes that occurred after the interview seemed particularly relevant to the story.

Each story in the book is unique and reflects the varied life experiences of the individual I interviewed. At the same time I discovered some common themes related to the sources of inspiration that influenced each person's ultimate sense of purpose. These common themes are the basis for the seven chapters which make up the book. The book begins with five individuals who were inspired to launch their nonprofit work by a life-changing event. It concludes with four individuals whose stories reflect a passion for setting aside convention and embracing new approaches to leadership.

Finally, I strove to reflect Oregon's demographic diversity. The stories represent a balance of ethnic, gender, nonprofit sector, and geographic community. Collectively, they form a mosaic that reflects the state of Oregon.

Despite their unique life stories, virtually all the people I interviewed have experienced some common circumstances that have defined their lives and their work. Relentless dedication to a cause does not come solely from academic knowledge, nor can it be created by carefully following best-practice recipes for leadership. Instead, it emerges through the impact of events and people along life's journey. These become the building blocks that create the foundation for success—a strong sense of purpose.

I

Life Changing Events

While many of the leaders I interviewed described life events that inspired them to pursue their nonprofit careers, a few stories stand out as particularly powerful. Whether tragic, strange, terrifying, or simply fortuitous, each of the events described by the leaders in this chapter not only altered the life of one person, but also set in motion a series of decisions that changed countless lives.

The Fighter
Alberto Moreno walked through an open door with the intention of stealing something. Instead, he discovered a boxing ring where he met a man who trained him to box and to stand up, not only for himself, but for others in the Latino community.

The Calling
For **Father Dick Berg**, a chance encounter with a "street angel" answered his prayer and set him on a mission of urban healing in Portland.

The Organizer
Marcy Westerling was kidnapped and sexually assaulted in Italy during her senior year abroad. Refusing to remain silent, Marcy took the case to court and won, inspiring her to become a lifelong advocate for social justice.

The Point Guard
After **Tony Hopson** came within seconds of accidentally shooting himself during his sophomore year of high school, he realized that God had a plan for him: to take responsibility for doing good in the community.

The Outsider
Growing up as a biracial child in a conservative Anglo community, **Andrea Williams** often struggled with the question, "What am I?" When she gave a speech about gay marriage in high school and visited a Mexican border town in college, she discovered her identity and became a champion of others facing the same struggle.

The Fighter

"Hunger, solitude and adversity are all teachers."

Alberto Moreno
August 2012

Alberto Moreno recalls the days when he was eight years old living in a small village of sixty families in the Sierra Madre Mountains of Mexico. His father was a subsistence corn farmer who would borrow teams of horses to plough the fields while Alberto sowed seeds. The family had no running water and never saw any cars driving through the village.

One year, disaster struck the farm, and all of the family's crops failed. This was followed by another crop failure the following year. The family had a choice: starve or emigrate.

Alberto's father moved to Chicago. Alberto, his four siblings and his mother followed two years later. They were all undocumented. All seven family members shared a dismal one-room apartment in a tenement building with only one toilet. They also shared a single shower with seven other large families in the building.

Life in Chicago made Alberto's home in the mountains seem like a paradise. Struggling to fit in, he joined a gang, the Latin Kings, at age 14. A life of crime loomed on the horizon for Alberto.

"One day I saw an open door and I went in, thinking I could steal something. But what I found instead was a room full of boxers sparring." He wandered over to a punching bag and started taking out his frustration on the bag. A man tapped him on the shoulder. Alberto was momentarily startled, but something in the man's expression caused Alberto to trust him. He then asked Alberto a life-changing question: "Do you want to learn how to box?"

"Clark taught me how to box. He trained me for two years. He saved my life, and I never even knew his last name," Alberto remembers.

With boxing providing a focus in his life, Alberto left the gang and became a Golden Gloves boxer. He also became interested in school for the first time in his life. "No one from my family had ever gone to college. At my high school there were 293 high school grads out of 3,000 students, and only six went to college."

Alberto's curiosity had come alive. He became a voracious reader, regularly going to the library to devour thick books. But his motivation to learn came from within, not from the school. One day the head librarian came over to him and, pointing to the book he was checking out, told him, "If you wait a couple weeks, the movie will be out!" Alberto checked out the book anyway.

He took the ACT test and scored higher than anyone at his high school had in 10 years. He had a dream of going to college, so he went to the school's guidance counselor. But instead of helping him, the counselor questioned whether he should apply for scholarships. "Aren't you illegal?" she said. Alberto stood up, looked the counselor directly in the eyes and said, "You yourself said these scholarships were merit-based. If there is nothing else to discuss, this conversation is ended." He walked out the door.

Years later, Alberto refers to the librarian and the guidance counselor as two of his most important teachers. His advice to others who face the same kind of challenges in life that he faced is clear: "Don't let somebody else's vision for you substitute for your vision for yourself."

The lack of support from Alberto's "teachers" inspired him to work even harder, and he ended up receiving four scholarship offers, including one to the University of Chicago and another to the University of Illinois. He attended the University of Illinois at Urbana but dropped out, unprepared for college life.

After going to a community college, he re-enrolled at Urbana and this time succeeded, receiving a BA in psychology. He became a social worker in Chicago and later went on to get his MSW. In spite of his academic success, he still felt aimless and missed climbing the mountains of his youth. With just a few dollars in his pocket, he tied the scant possessions he had to the back of his motorcycle and headed for the Northwest.

Landing in southwest Washington, he became a bilingual, bicultural counselor and started the region's first migrant clinic. He loved the cause, but he hated administration, so he left for Oregon, where he got a job with the state as a migrant health coordinator.

Alberto was inspired by the challenge of tackling the health disparities that existed in Oregon, where 176,000 migrant and seasonal farmworkers had an average life expectancy of fewer than 49 years.

Despite his success at reaching out to this population, he resented the restrictions that came with being a government employee. On the one hand, he was charged with supporting people in great need. At the same time, he wasn't allowed to advocate for policies that would improve their lives. As Alberto wryly observes, "I was not paid for my voice, but for my silence."

In 2012, he left his state job and started a nonprofit group, the Oregon Latino Health Coalition. His number-one goal was to serve undocumented women who were ineligible for prenatal care. Because these women could not receive the care they needed, their infant mortality rate was 25% higher than the state average.

With a staff of two and a budget of only $50,000 in 2012, Alberto worked tirelessly to make prenatal care a human right in Oregon. By 2014, over 50,000 women and children had received prenatal care, with millions of dollars in federal funds leveraged for health care. In April 2014, Alberto was appointed by Governor Kitzhaber to serve as chair of the Commission on

Hispanic Affairs for the State of Oregon. In this capacity, he continues to advocate for the needs of Latinos in Oregon.

For Alberto, arriving at this point has been a long journey fraught with hunger, adversity and solitude. But throughout this journey—from poor, undocumented immigrant to dismissed scholar and on to stifled counselor—Alberto's fighting spirit has continued to push him forward. And now, it seems, his voice is finally being heard.

The Calling

"I asked God to help me figure out what to do with my new job. The street angel came to give me the answer."

Father Dick Berg
July 2010

Imagine it's 1989. You are walking through Old Town in Portland, Oregon. As you begin to pass by the Starry Night, the most popular music venue in town (some say it's also haunted), you notice a group of curious people gathered at the street corner. You wander over to observe a tall priest standing over a tiny, frail, elderly man. The man is kneeling and holding crutches. The priest, with one hand on the man's head and the other on his shoulder, is praying gently to God for relief of his pain and suffering. No sooner has the priest helped him to his feet than this same man looks straight up at the priest and says, "That was a fine prayer, pastor. Now you get down, and I'll pray for you."

The priest kneels down nervously as the elderly man slowly gets to his feet. "Dear God," he prays. "This new pastor doesn't know much about what's going on here. I pray that he brings healing to our city. Amen." By the time the priest looks up to thank him, the man has already gone around the corner and is out of sight. The priest and the crowd look around the corner, but he has disappeared.

That tall priest was Father Dick Berg. As a young man of 17, Dick was "hit like a wallop" to become a priest. He shared this dream with his father, an orthopedic surgeon, who advised him to first attend church for nine consecutive days. His father understood both Dick's enthusiastic nature and his chronic disinterest in attending church. Dick reluctantly followed his father's advice, but never set aside his dreams of the priesthood. "I always wanted to be a priest-teacher."

Dick attended seminary at Notre Dame, was ordained in Rome, and then went on to obtain his doctorate in psychology. But after finishing school, he felt burnt out and lost. One day he decided to retreat into the woods to ask God for energy and direction. As he was waiting for a response, he recalls, "Suddenly, warmth and light filled my body, and I began singing."

After completing his postdoctoral work, Dick followed his inspiration, teaching full time and setting up a household for the homeless in Texas. While he was there, he did all the cooking and says he experienced "the gift of healing." But his journey had only just begun. The search for his calling eventually led Dick to Oregon, where he continued teaching and served as a religious superior. In Portland he took on a "temporary position" as dean of arts and sciences at the University of Portland that lasted 13 years!

Then, in 1989, he received an urgent call from the archdiocese. Dick was asked to serve as pastor of Portland's St. Vincent de Paul Downtown Chapel. Although he felt conflicted about being a dean and a pastor at the same time, he was told, "You can be dean by day and pastor by night."

Dick's heart was filled with questions, but he felt compelled to accept this additional call to pastoral ministry, reflecting on the gift that he felt God had given him years earlier in serving the homeless in Texas. He moved to the Downtown Chapel, but didn't fully comprehend the enormity of the challenge. With 21 hotels for the very poor, drug dealers everywhere, and police and ambulance sirens filling the air day and night, he felt lost in an urban wilderness, with no confidence that he could change the established disorder.

On his first night on the job, after he was awakened for the fourth time, he got dressed and went downstairs to the chapel. Dick recalls thinking, "I'd better speak to God about this situation I've gotten myself into. What on Earth can I do here in the heart of such complex and urgent needs?" He prayed for guidance and then, exhausted, went back upstairs to sleep.

One week later, Dick was walking in front of the Starry Night when he encountered the elderly man with crutches. Now, when he tells this story, he thanks the "street angel" who answered his prayer and set him on a mission of urban healing in Portland. After two years of trying to be both a dean and priest, Dick left his academic post and put the full force of his energy into his call to urban healing.

Early in his ministry, a Jewish doctor who served the homeless at a clinic on Burnside Street in depressed Old Town Portland asked Dick for help. He explained how the clinic was able to provide the homeless with medical assistance, while soup kitchens and hotels were meeting their needs for food and shelter. What his clients lacked, said the doctor, was support for their social needs to allow them to become productive members of society.

So Dick approached Hal Westby, a colleague from the University of Portland's development office, and asked for help. He credits Hal with providing him with the gift of "skepticism and tough questions." This was just what Dick needed. By expressing doubt that Dick would be able to do anything to improve the desperate plight of the Old Town homeless, Westby made him all the more determined to do something. Dick reflects, "The more people say it can't be done, the harder I try!" The same entrepreneurial spirit that inspired Dick to establish a parakeet business as a schoolboy got him off his feet and diving into a new project: to develop a center for the urban poor and homeless in downtown Portland.

He then approached a family friend, Maybelle Clark Macdonald, who later passed away in 2009 at the age of 93, leaving a legacy of philanthropic support for education, the arts, and services to Oregon's most vulnerable populations. She was inspired by his vision and made a $1 million pledge. Dick then told Hal Westby of the pledge and reiterated his determination and the serious nature of his quest. At that point, Hal became convinced that his friend had a chance to succeed where many had failed. He committed to working with Dick, and together they raised the money to purchase property for the center.

Dick tells me the story of a banker who initially opposed the idea of "spending millions of dollars to care for people who contribute nothing to society." Whether it was Dick's explanation of Thomas Kelly's *Doctrine of Inner Light*, or simply Dick's tenacious sense of purpose, the banker eventually relented and became one of the initial supporters of the center.

In 1999, five years after the first Macdonald pledge and $6.5 million later, the Macdonald Center for the frail, poor and homeless (now called the Maybelle Center for Community) became a reality. With private donors, foundations and tax credits financing the facility, and with Medicaid paying for operational support, Fr. Dick Berg's dream had been realized!

The Organizer

> "Small town Americana is filled with justice-seeking souls that deserve support as well as to have the power to bridge the false cultural divides of our times. There's a lot to be done on this journey called life and this journey toward justice...Count me in."
>
> Marcy Westerling
June 2012

It's a typical June day in Portland, when the sun just can't work up the strength to break through the gray. As I approach the home of Marcy Westerling, I have mixed emotions. Marcy had told me that she has stage IV cancer and that I should not wear any scent; furthermore, she could not predict how long her strength would hold out. At the same time, Ramon Ramirez, the highly respected president of the Northwest Farmworkers Union, had suggested just one name for me to interview—Marcy Westerling. So I am both anxious and intrigued when I sit down across from Marcy on her backyard patio and begin asking questions.

Marcy describes her childhood as that of a "protected, privileged, young white gal in a traditional, apolitical family in a small Long Island town." She traces her identity as an organizer to her Dutch ancestry, speaking fondly of her grandfather, who was a resistance organizer in occupied Holland. "While my grandfather had been a true hero who saved many lives while risking his own, he was just a decent man with backbone." As she grew up, Marcy didn't fully realize the influence her grandfather had on her life. She remained apolitical, attending an elite Ivy League college, where she ranked near the top of her class.

As the interview continues, Marcy goes on to talk about her work with ACORN (Association of Community Organizations for Reform Now). After she speaks for several minutes, I reflect on how unusual it is for someone from her background to go to work for an organization with such a strong political leaning. I ask her what could have possibly happened to create such a dramatic change in the course of her life. She pauses and is silent for a very long moment. Then she begins a story that she had no intention of telling.

During her junior year abroad in Italy, Marcy was kidnapped and sexually assaulted. In spite of her trauma and plea for help, her school did not support her. At the time, rape was an epidemic in the community where she lived. Many women who had been raped but had remained silent approached Marcy and gave her support. Marcy felt she was a part of something bigger than just herself, so she decided to take the case to court. With the help of other rape victims, she won the case, and her life changed forever.

When she returned to college, Marcy continued her advocacy work, surveying women students and conducting seminars on how to avoid rape. Upon graduation, she knew she could not go home, where her family was falling apart from a bitter divorce. Instead, she moved to Minneapolis to live with her best friend.

Her experiences organizing in Italy and at college inspired her to apply for a job with ACORN. They didn't immediately hire her, but the "fire in [her] belly" drove her to create a position for herself as a community organizer, and she began working 80 hours a week and raising her own salary. After five years in the Midwest working for ACORN and at an institution for violence-prone men with cognitive disabilities, she was hired to serve victims of domestic abuse through a women's resource center in Scappoose, Oregon. She approached this work with the same ferocious determination as her work with ACORN, and she ultimately became president of the statewide battered women's coalition.

Up to this point, Marcy's intense focus on her work had kept her from getting involved in the life of this small Oregon community. That all changed one day, when a friend invited her to attend a school board meeting. The board was going to decide whether to endorse a creationist curriculum for the schools. Marcy was alarmed when she heard about this development, and she decided she needed to be there. Of the 300 people who attended that meeting, about half strongly supported the creationist curriculum, while the other half (including Marcy) were strongly opposed to it. The board voted against the curriculum, but only by a razor-thin, one-vote margin.

Marcy reflects, "Based on that experience, I decided we needed to organize!" Not long after the board meeting, she got involved in the community and was instrumental in creating the Columbia County Coalition for Human Dignity. Believing that every rural community in Oregon needed an organization which was willing and able to take a stand on difficult social issues, Marcy contacted her colleagues from domestic violence organizations around the state and offered to help if they would set up organizational meetings.

When a conservative Christian political action group, the Oregon Citizens Alliance, launched the anti-gay Ballot Measure 9, she led a grassroots effort to defeat it. Despite anti-Measure 9 organizers facing strong opposition and even death threats, there was an enormous response and the measure was defeated.

The defeat of Measure 9 inspired Marcy to found the Rural Organizing Project (ROP), which she led, in addition to working her other job, on a starting budget of $18,000. From 1992 to 2012, the budget of ROP did not increase much (funding only three full-time organizers), but the impact of the Project was significant. Over forty human dignity organizations have sprung up around the state, and ROP has engaged in many projects, including organizing rural Latino leadership retreats, fighting post office closures, and championing immigration reform.

At the time of our interview in 2012, as she struggles with stage IV ovarian cancer, Marcy is hard at work documenting the work ROP has taken on over the past two decades. She regrets that the many visits from out-of-state groups to learn about and replicate the ROP model have produced few lasting results. Other states were too staff-intensive in their approach and unable to duplicate ROP's low-budget, high-dedication model. But she remains upbeat.

"Statistically, I am doomed," she says. "I have been handed my pink slip from the world. But the crazy thing is, I am doing fine. I stay very happy and very hopeful—traits I have learned in pursuit of justice. Early on, I wrote a little test obituary:"

> *Marcy Westerling: A kick-ass community organizer dedicated to the notion that small town Americana is filled with justice-seeking souls that deserve support as well as to have the power to bridge the false cultural divides of our times. Derailed by stage IV ovarian cancer in spring 2010, I trust others to move rural, inclusive, progressive organizing forward.*

Later, in 2014 she added, "The only thing I would change is inserting 'momentarily' before 'derailed.' There's a lot to be done on this journey called life and this journey toward justice…Count me in."

Author's note: On June 10, 2015, Marcy died of ovarian cancer, having inspired countless followers around the world through her blog, "Livingly Dying: Notes and Essays on Daily Life with Terminal Cancer."

The Point Guard

> "We need high standards for all children. We need to put our last name on every child."
>
> Tony Hopson, Sr.
> June 2012

When reflecting upon his life, Tony Hopson tells a story from when he was a sophomore in high school. At that time, his father was working late at night and always carried a pistol with him. One day his father came home and then was abruptly called away on an emergency. Tony noticed the pistol on the pull-out bed in their dining room. He didn't think it was a real gun because it had a broken handle. Besides, there was no reason a loaded gun would be left around the house. As he ate his cereal, Tony played with the gun, leaning it against his temple. Moments later, the gun fired—just after he had moved it away from his head. Tony remembers the incident:

> *I felt that in many ways I was supposed to die that day. But from that point on I felt like, "God has some serious plans for you." That kind of added to directing my work and directing my heart toward knowing that I am here for*

a very special reason, and that I need to own that and the responsibility for doing good.

Tony Hopson is a Portland native. He was raised by a family that was "rich spiritually but not financially." His father was a custodian who worked two or three jobs at a time. "He worked himself to death," reflects Tony.

Tony, his two brothers and three sisters would all go to work with their father, which fostered a solid work ethic in each of the six siblings. Tony later attended Jefferson High School, where he excelled as an athlete. While he was a student there, the population of the school shifted from a white majority to a black majority. In his senior year in 1972, Tony was a point guard on the nearly undefeated (26-1) Jefferson High basketball team. Yet he still harbors vivid memories of racist incidents which occurred as he and his teammates traveled around the state, most notably the time that a riot broke out at Benson High School.

In the face of all these challenges, the community rallied around the team and its players during that 1972 championship year. Afterward, Tony felt a deep sense of gratitude for all of the support he received. He decided, "I need to give back to my community."

The truth is that Tony Hopson had been "giving back" long before 1972. At age 13, he began organizing summer programs for elementary students at Peninsula Park. At the age of 15 he was running the Jefferson Gym program for high school and college students, most of whom were older than he was. These experiences set the course for his career in community service.

In addition, for Tony, the Civil Rights Movement of the '60s and '70s served as an inspiration and a call to action. "Kennedy was shot. Martin Luther King Jr. and Malcolm X were assassinated. All these things played heavily into shaping my thoughts. I asked myself, 'Are you going to be part of the problem or part of the solution?'"

Given the fact that he was not a great student, Tony saw basketball as his vehicle to get into the NBA and make his mark on the world. That aspiration motivated him to pursue college. After a two-year stint at Mt. Hood Community College, Tony went on to Morehead State and then to Willamette University, where he completed his BA. He later received a counseling and teaching certificate from Portland State University.

He continued to play basketball in college and even had an opportunity to try out with the Portland Trail Blazers rookie camp in 1977—the year they won the national championship. Although he was not destined to play in the NBA, basketball would continue to play an important role in his life.

After graduating from college, Tony worked as a teacher at Portland Public Schools for 10 years. This period included four years as a Title VII coordinator, where he worked with students of color who were bussed to Lincoln High School, three years as a freshman-sophomore counselor at Jefferson High School, and three years directing the Achievement Athletic Motivation Program in four Portland public high schools.

In 1981 he started Self Enhancement Camp. It began as a one-week camp with the goal of transferring the lessons that sports teach to the classroom. The emphasis was 50% sports and 50%

academics. The program grew each year between 1981 and 1988.

Then, in 1988, there was a gang-related drive-by shooting which tragically took the life of a young man. One of the shooters and the victim were both participants in Self Enhancement Camp. The victim of this Crips and Bloods rivalry lived in a violence prone community. Tony had worked hard to talk this young man out of gang activity, but he respectfully rejected Tony's advice. He knew he needed to make money and support his family, and he felt that being a member of a gang was the only way to do it.

This incident pushed the City of Portland to fund Tony's program year-round. Tony then left the school district, which transferred funds to support the program. Superintendent Matthew Prophet knew that there was a gap between what the school could do and what these youths needed, and he believed in Tony Hopson.

"All this was a spiritual experience for me. Self Enhancement came to me. I had my plan. And God had his plan for me. I was blessed to know what I wanted to do from an early age."

Tony and three other staff members first expanded Self Enhancement Inc. (SEI) to Jefferson High School and its three feeder middle schools, and then expanded it at the elementary level. According to Tony, "Kids need a caring influence in their lives, and SEI became an extension of the family and a bridge between home and school."

For Tony, this effort became more than a just a job; it became a lifestyle. In his work he is driven by a set of values that focuses on community service. Leadership becomes bigger than any single person; the leader must embody the culture. "We need high standards for all children," he says. "We need to put our last name on every child."

Over the last third of a century, SEI has served thousands of young people. Tony is proud of SEI's accomplishments. The program pairs each at-risk student with a paid SEI coordinator who is available 24-7 to help guide, support and enhance the student's life. The coordinator is fully engaged with the student from age 8 to 25.

Each student develops a success plan. Success at SEI has been very real and measurable: 96% of students have graduated from high school, and 85% have gone on to college. By 2015, the program was impacting the lives of over 7,500 children, families and adults each year.

One of Tony's proudest achievements was the construction of the Center for Self Enhancement in 1997. This 62,000 square-foot facility includes a gymnasium, performing arts auditorium, dance studio, library, computer lab and science lab. The building is located in a neighborhood with a history of crime and gang violence.

Before construction began, Tony and others sat down with members of the Kerby Street Crips, the gang in control of the neighborhood at the time. He talked with gang members about SEI's mission and enlisted their support for the project. In return, the Crips protected the building while it was under construction. To date this building has never been tagged or vandalized by gang members.

Despite his achievements, Tony is still concerned about the future. He cites the prediction that by 2023 more than half of the children in this country will come from ethnic minority groups. "I can turn 1,000 kids around. But there are ten for every one we can help." Like Matthew Prophet, Tony believes that the school district cannot educate our children on its own. Educating children includes home, community and school.

When I ask what needs to happen in each student's life to make the program a success, Tony responds:

> *Every student will become a PCC (positive, contributing citizen) when we can help all kids find their gift by providing options and opportunities for success. This will happen when we realize that we don't have a youth problem in America; we have an adult problem.*

As we end the interview, Tony again reflects on his near-miss with the pistol and on God's plan for him. He believes that God also has a plan for every SEI student. "Both the problem and the solution stare back at us in the mirror every day. Every one of us has a gift, and we need to share that gift as far and as wide as we can."

The Outsider

"Sometimes you have to ask your ancestors, 'Give me wisdom!'"

Andrea Williams
September 2017

As we begin the interview, I explain to Andrea Williams the purpose of my book: to shine a light on Oregon nonprofit leaders and gain insight into what inspired them to do the work they do—the people, the events, and the stories.

She immediately begins describing an event which occurred in 2004, when she was 15 years old. That year Oregonians passed Ballot Measure 36, an anti-gay marriage initiative. Andrea felt so strongly about the measure that she made a speech at school about LGBTQ rights. Her parents disagreed with gay marriage and told Andrea that it was a sin and unnatural. Not knowing how to argue, she yelled and stomped out of the room.

When I ask what inspired her to go against her parents' opinions, Andrea explains, "I wasn't very political in high school. I was a member of the business club DECA. When I did the speech,

I was driven by compassion for other people." As a teenager, Andrea's cousin came out as gay to his mother and was kicked out of the house.

Andrea describes herself as a millennial who grew up in a south Salem community that was made up largely of conservative white Christians. Most of her classmates, like her parents, gave her "a lot of flack" for her speech and attitude toward LGBTQ people. Some of her classmates avoided her after the speech, and one student even tried to convert her to Christianity.

She continues:

> *One reason I saw the world differently from my classmates is that I am multiracial. My dad is white and my mom is Filipino/Japanese. As I grew up, I was constantly asked "what" I was. People perceived me differently from the rest. When I was little and trying to discover my identity, it was traumatizing to be asked what I was, because I saw myself just like anyone else. When I took standardized tests, I was asked about my race and had to fill in a multiple choice bubble. What am I? I put Pacific Islander. When I came home from school that day, I asked my mom and she laughed at me and said, "You are Asian." I felt embarrassed that I chose the wrong race, and I also felt confused. Unfortunately, we didn't talk about these things openly in my family, and I didn't have any other peers to relate to at that time.*

Today, Andrea Williams is executive director of a Salem-based immigrants' rights organization Causa, which addresses issues facing Oregon's Latino immigrant community. Responding to what led her to take this path, she reflects:

Maybe my empathy for other minority groups comes from the fact that I did not feel that I belonged. Because I was asked so often what I was, it motivated me to probe deeply into my past. I had to ask questions over and over again from my family to better understand my roots.

Andrea goes on to describe her roots:

I don't know much about my dad's side. His dad—my grandfather— left for the army, and my dad grew up with a single mom—my grandmother—a waitress on government assistance who struggled to make ends meet. She married five different times, gave birth to three children and gave one up for adoption. Dad never stayed at one school for long; they were always moving. My grandmother's last husband moved the family to Hawaii for a construction job.

Andrea becomes animated when she describes her mother's side of the family:

I am much closer to my mom's side. I visit my family in Maui often. I grew up in Oregon, but loved it when my big Hawaiian family came to visit. I was so proud to hang out with them. It made me feel part of something…part of a whole.

Andrea's great-grandfather on her mother's side, Atanacio Ramos Tabbal, emigrated from the Philippines in the 1920s to work in the sugar cane fields of Hawaii. He was a union member and leader and came across as very intimidating. He married a Japanese woman, Chiyoko Mashiba, who left an arranged marriage to be with him. Leaving a Japanese husband for a Filipino man was a big deal back then, and her family disowned her. Chiyoko had a total of 13 children, with 11 of them from her marriage with Atanacio.

Prior to Andrea's mother's generation, all the family members worked in the fields or the hotels. When Hawaii became a state, they were naturalized as US citizens, since at that time the Philippines was recognized as a territory of the US. Andrea smiles, "I still have pictures of my great-grandparents when they received their citizenship. They were lucky!"

Andrea's grandfather, Rudolpho (Rudy) Tabbal made it from field worker to manager of the sugar cane factory after Andrea's mother was born. He even supervised his own father, Atanacio Tabbal, who was a field worker for his entire life. As a supervisor, Rudy became very conservative, and often listened to Rush Limbaugh's radio show. His wife—Andrea's grandmother Florence—came from a family of Filipino immigrants who were also field workers. Florence and Rudy were both born and raised on the plantation camp, where they met.

Florence eventually moved on from field work and became a hotel worker and house cleaner. She also became a union leader as a shop steward, fighting for better wages and benefits for her fellow hotel workers. Now in her 80s, Florence is still an active member of her union. Florence and Rudy divorced after most of their four kids grew up and moved out of the house.

Despite mixed political views throughout the generations, Andrea grew up in a nuclear family that was politically conservative. Andrea talks about her parents, who married at the age of 19 and moved from Maui to Kelso, Washington, seeking a better education and more opportunities:

> *They both worked hard to support themselves and put each other through college—my mom held off on getting a college degree, helping to pay for my dad's education. Later, in their 40s, my dad helped my mom get her bachelor's degree. They were both believers in hard work and the "pulling yourself up by your bootstraps" mentality.*

Although Andrea's independent spirit showed itself in her high school speech, she describes her experience at Whitman College in Walla Walla, Washington as the turning point in developing her political consciousness.

As a freshman she had a life-changing experience. She applied to a school program that gave her the opportunity to spend a week on the Mexican/US border learning about immigration issues. The Mexican family she stayed with lived just across the border in a house with dirt floors. The house was set against a group of large factories, where companies hired cheap local labor. Andrea toured the factories and interviewed workers and managers.

According to Andrea, "Staying with the family broke my heart. I didn't realize what living conditions were like. I saw extreme poverty and it changed my worldview. The trip inspired me to study politics and immigration."

Andrea spent spring break traveling in Oregon and Washington to learn about immigration issues in the Northwest. During that trip, she toured the Tacoma Detention Center and talked with ICE officials and members of anti-immigrant groups. She also stayed with farmworkers and talked with representatives of PCUN (Northwest Farmworkers Union). At this time Oregon Governor Ted Kulongoski was taking driver's licenses away from undocumented workers.

In the summer of 2008, Andrea discovered Causa, a Salem-based immigration rights organization. She got involved as an intern registering voters and was eventually hired as a grant writer. Upon graduation from Whitman College in 2009 she became a full-time Causa staffer.

In Causa she found her calling:

> *I wanted to give back to the community. I told them I would do anything they needed. I began as a fundraiser, organizing their first gala event. My dad is a lobbyist for Weyerhaeuser. We were often on opposite sides of the same bill—for example, minimum wage—but on immigration, we were on the same side.*

At that time, Causa was a small team of three or four employees, but it grew quickly. In 2011, she became associate director at the age of 23. Eventually she and the executive director disagreed, and she moved on to work for another organization. But when the executive director position opened up in 2013, she applied.

She was both excited and conflicted about the opportunity. "I hesitated because I thought Causa should be led by a Latino. Finally, my husband and PCUN Executive Director, Ramon Ramirez, convinced me to apply, and I was accepted."

Describing her four years of leading Causa, Andrea reflects,

"Working at Causa has been a total rollercoaster ride! We have achieved many victories, but we have also suffered many painful losses."

During her first year, the legislature passed a law granting driver's cards to undocumented residents. The following year, an anti-immigrant group passed Ballot Measure 88, overturning the law. Andrea was immediately thrown into a high level of visibility. "The Measure 88 campaign was a huge learning experience for me. I was new to politics and approached the campaign from a very rational perspective. We lost by a large margin."

Andrea was at the Democratic Party of Oregon's election night event and was prepared to give a speech. Shortly before the speech, she found out the result of Measure 88. She had what she refers to as a nervous breakdown, losing all feeling in her hands and face.

> *It was the hardest moment in my career at Causa. The lopsided defeat taught us that we had to lead with our hearts and not just our heads. The next day the staff bounced back. I've never seen people so resilient in my life.*

Andrea describes losing DACA (Deferred Action for Childhood Arrivals) in September 2017:

> *It was the second hardest day of my life. We fought hard for DACA and the driver's card. On both occasions we won and then had the victories taken away. Both experiences were traumatizing, but we responded the same way each time: we got back to work and coped by being busy.*

Comparing the different responses to the 2016 presidential election, Andrea observes:

> The people who struggled the most at first with Donald Trump's victory were white folks. The groups representing minorities and people of color bounced right back. White groups wanted to mourn and process. We wanted to move forward. You become good at losing and picking yourself up.

In spite of the difficult losses, Andrea finds hope in the recent wins—minimum wage, paid sick leave, health care for undocumented children:

> We killed three anti-immigrant ballot measures headed for the 2016 election. We came back stronger and wiser. Now we feel that we are closer than ever, and yet still so far, from something we have worked so hard for. Elected leaders have had their eyes opened wide. Both Ds and Rs are becoming champions of immigration issues. But there is still so much left to do!

After the DACA loss, Andrea asked her 85-year-old grandmother, "Did you ever win?" She answered, "Yes! We went on strike, and won better benefits for the workers."

"I needed that," Andrea exclaims. "Sometimes you have to ask your ancestors, 'Give me wisdom!'"

As our interview comes to an end, I ask Andrea what advice her great grandfather would give her. Her response: "Atanacio would say, 'Keep fighting, girl!'"

II

Overcoming Barriers

We often think of barriers as insurmountable roadblocks on the way to achieving success. They can stop us dead in our tracks or even turn us away. Paradoxically, for the following nonprofit leaders, those very barriers were not a hindrance, but served as the motivation for each to succeed.

The Mentor
Duncan Campbell grew up with alcoholic parents and no positive adult role models. Lacking a mentor himself, his faith led him to find mentors for hundreds of children like him.

The Reformer
Paul Solomon survived a broken family and a life of drugs and prison before he turned his life around and dedicated it to others who face similar challenges.

The Sister
Genny Nelson overcame type 1 diabetes and a crippling sense of unworthiness by founding a cafe that helped others find an affordable meal and discover dignity in their lives.

The Storyteller
Trish Seiler survived a difficult childhood, including a volatile home life and a severe physical handicap, to become an influential leader by helping her community tell its story.

The Rebel
Michael Eichman overcame the stigma of his last name and a strict disciplinarian upbringing on a dryland farm in eastern Colorado. He was a rebel who left home, found his purpose and became a force for good in the world.

The Mentor

> "People thought I had a mentor...Actually, it was because I did not have a mentor that I wanted others to have one."
>
> Duncan Campbell
> November 2012

The room is filled with excitement and expectation as a group of eight-year-old boys gathers together. Parents mingle in the crowd. One boy, Duncan Campbell, looks nervously around the room and toward the entry door. The Cub Scout initiation is about to begin, and Duncan's father is nowhere to be seen. The ceremony begins. Each boy, accompanied by his father, is sworn in to the troop. Duncan is the only boy who is alone. His downcast eyes and a hardly noticeable tear are lost among the smiling faces. As the ceremony ends, Duncan moves quickly to the exit, only to encounter his father, staggering in and slurring, "I'm here. Everything's ok." But it wasn't ok for Duncan.

Duncan Campbell grew up on 10th and Alberta in Northeast Portland in a dysfunctional welfare family. His father was in prison twice while he was growing up. "I was left alone to raise myself. My parents never helped me with my homework, never came to my games. I can't remember many enjoyable things we ever did together."

He remembers wandering the streets of Portland at the age of three, with his pants inside out, looking for his parents. The nightmare seemed to last forever, until he was finally picked up by the police, who found his parents in a nearby tavern.

Duncan's life experience showed him that children very often follow in the footsteps of their parents. This could have easily been Duncan's story. But he describes that day at the Cub Scout ceremony as "the straw that broke the camel's back." Not long after that incident, Duncan had another vivid memory. He was sitting alone and thinking about his life. "It was an epiphany. I was in the basement doing laundry. I remember the moment that it became very clear to me that I was not going to live like my parents."

From that day on, his life changed forever. He never had a drink in high school or in college. "People thought I had a mentor. The closest thing I had to a mentor was a fifth grade teacher and a football coach. Actually, it was because I did not have a mentor that I wanted others to have one."

After graduating from high school, Duncan received scholarships and worked multiple part-time jobs to attend Portland State University. While he was in college, his mother died due to alcohol-related problems, followed several years later by his father. He started law school three times before he finally finished at the University of Oregon and became a lawyer. In his early twenties, while he was working at the juvenile court, he often wondered whether some of the kids would be there at all if they just had a friend.

Following his work at juvenile court, he began his business career as a CPA with Arthur Anderson and later founded a timber investment firm, the Campbell Group. At the time, the forest industry was suffering from a down economy and a low return on land. Duncan saw an opportunity and was able to persuade large institutional investors to put their money into timberland. The arrangement turned out to be successful for all parties—timberland owners, investors and the Campbell Group. By 2012, the Campbell Group was responsible for managing over 3.1 million acres of land worldwide.

Despite the extraordinary success of the Campbell Group, Duncan Campbell felt a different calling. Ever since that moment in the basement, he had promised himself that if he ever became wealthy, he would use his money to help children who had grown up in homes like his. He couldn't stop thinking about those kids in juvenile court. If only they had a friend…

Those thoughts led Duncan, in 1993, to begin a seven-year process of transitioning control of his business and starting a new career as founder of Friends of the Children. Duncan tells his story:

> *I met Dr. Orin Bolstad from Morrison Child and Family Services. He was the first executive director of the Children's Institute and helped create the model for Friends of the Children. I had this idea: let's hire three friends and pick 24 children.*

But Duncan didn't start Friends of the Children based solely on his gut feelings. He also funded a two-year research project which showed that early intervention and the involvement of adult mentors makes a difference. He explains:

> *At Friends of the Children, we start at kindergarten and work with causes, not symptoms. We carefully select the most difficult children, those who have accumulated the most heartache and trouble in their early years. 85% of children replicate the behavior of their caregivers/family. That's why pairing kids with friends is so important.*

At Friends of the Children, participants are carefully screened through six weeks of observation before being selected. Mentors begin with children in kindergarten and follow them through high school. Given the high-risk nature of the children chosen, the program has achieved extraordinary results. 85% of participants graduate from high school, 92% avoid the juvenile justice system, and 98% avoid teen pregnancy. These numbers contrast markedly with non-participating children from similar backgrounds. Furthermore, a return-on-investment study showed a $7 return for each dollar invested in the program.

The "friend" deals not only with school performance, but all aspects of a child's life. Friends are paid a salary and spend at least four hours per week with each child they support. Duncan credits the professionalism of dedicated paid staff with much of the program's success.

> *We assume that the parents of our kids want to be good parents. We are not parents and are not social workers, nor do we pay rent or bills. Boundaries are very important. The friend becomes a mentor not only to the kids but also to*

their parents, especially the mothers.

Duncan finds much of his inspiration through a deep faith:

> *At age 30 I was an agnostic. Ten years later I found Christ. I turned to Christ over a two-year period, beginning with Bible study. God said to me, "It doesn't make any difference what anyone in the world does. It is your relationship with me."*

The same philosophy that made Duncan so successful in business carried over to his work in the nonprofit sector.

> *I am a big risk-taker. But my favorite word is balance. I am passionate about having a plan, but I am willing to adapt, change and learn from mistakes. My goal is to change one child's life. And if I can change one child's life, maybe I can change 1,000 children's lives.*

He is doing it. In 2012, over 90 friends served over 700 children in Portland, Klamath Falls, Seattle, Boston and New York. New programs were in the process of being established in Tampa Bay and Cornwall, England.

Duncan Campbell has earned the adulation of his home town for his leadership in founding Friends of the Children. He received the Purpose Prize in 2009 and was named Portland First Citizen in 2012. He responds to this recognition with gratitude and humility.

> *It is clear to me that I am called to do this work. I have loved business, but this is a thousand times more rewarding.*

I wouldn't want anyone to have my childhood, but I am so fortunate to have had it, because it has given me the blessings I have now.

The Reformer

> "I made some mistakes many years ago, but that is not who I am. I don't want to be judged for the worst things I have ever done."
>
> Paul Solomon
> March 2015

On September 28, 2003, Paul Solomon stood proudly in the Gus J. Solomon Courthouse in Portland as he and his wife-to-be, Jennifer, exchanged vows of marriage. The courthouse bore the name of his grandfather, who served as Chief Judge of the United States District Court of Oregon from 1958 to 1971. That moment was significant for Paul on many levels. Fifteen years earlier, Paul sat in a room in the same courthouse and was sentenced to prison.

When I called Paul to set up the interview, he indicated that his story was "not a story I tell very often. I am someone who has overcome my background. It makes it easier for me to do this work."

Paul's mother and father (Gus's son) met in 1965 when they were freshmen at UC Santa Barbara. She was the first in her family to attend college. When she became pregnant with Paul in 1965, they moved back to Portland, where Paul's father had grown up. Because of the stigma associated with children born out of wedlock, they went out of the country to get married.

Back in his hometown, Paul's father protested the Vietnam War while going to school at Portland State University. In 1969, when Paul was three years old, his parents divorced, and Paul's mother married a man who later became a drug dealer.

Paul grew up living with his mother and stepfather but spent a lot of time traveling around the country with his grandparents. "It was a tumultuous upbringing. I lived in different worlds, but did fairly well despite the challenges at home. Due to my grandfather's influence, I was very involved with the Jewish community."

Around 1979, when Paul was 13 years old (shortly after his Bar Mitzvah), he started getting involved with drugs. He attended Jefferson High School and played basketball, but he dropped out of school and left home in his sophomore year. By age 15, he was strung out on heroin.

He started selling drugs and committing petty crimes. The first time he was arrested was for forgery in 1984. Later, he became involved in more serious crimes, culminating in his arrest in 1988 on charges of bank robbery. Following his sentencing in his grandfather's courthouse, he spent over eight years in prison.

Growing up in Northeast Portland as a Jewish kid with many black friends, he was not prepared for the racism and white supremacist gangs he encountered in prison.

> *I spent a lot of time in solitary confinement, as a result of fights and challenging authority. I understood due process, but in prison things work very differently. Because I grew up in a family with a strong history of activism, I challenged the things I thought were wrong.*

At that time in his life, Paul did not see any other future for himself. "My view of the world was myopic. My reality was that I had no choices."

Paul's years in prison were divided between the state and federal prison systems. During the five years that Paul was in federal prison in Sheridan, Oregon, he went to college and had access to a library and far more resources than he had when he was in the state system. His grandfather would write him letters until he passed away in 1987.

Ever since Paul was a teenager, he and his biological father had had a strained relationship. But after Paul was incarcerated, his father began visiting him regularly, and they renewed their relationship.

> *I realized that I needed to change my life. When I was in Sheridan, I began to mature. I took accounting classes and worked in the business office. But I still had one foot in prison life. A turning point for me was when I got in trouble for a dirty drug test—opiates.*

The drug test resulted in Paul being sentenced to spend an additional 60 days in solitary confinement, after already spending an entire year in isolation. "Everything that was going well was now at risk. At that point, I decided that I didn't want to spend the rest of my life in prison."

Fortunately for Paul, the business manager at the UNICOR furniture factory, where Paul worked at the prison, stood up for him and allowed him to keep his job. "I got out in 1993. That was the beginning of my life outside of crime."

Family friend, Jerry Kohlberg, founder of the private equity firm Kohlberg, Kravis and Roberts, suggested that Paul use his bookkeeping skills to get a job at Fred Meyer. He began at Fred Meyer as an entry level accounting clerk and worked his way up to a corporate tax specialist. He started volunteering with at-risk youth and served on the Fred Meyer volunteer council. These activities inspired him to do something different.

He began night school at PSU and in 1996 moved to Eugene, where he attended the University of Oregon full time, graduating cum laude with a BA in sociology. After graduation, Paul married, but trouble again found him. Shortly after getting married, he injured his back. To add insult to injury, his wife was having an affair. Paul relapsed, abusing the narcotics that had been prescribed for him.

> *I went back into the system for a short time, this time for selling drugs in Lane County. But I realized that I could do something different this time. I was miserable. It was a catalyst for a lifelong change. I never wanted to go back to the world of drugs and prison.*

Paul was working and applying to enter graduate school. One

day, as he was talking with his landlord, Paul shared with him certain details of his past. The next day he was asked to move out of his apartment.

Desperate to talk about the discrimination he had suffered and to learn about housing options, Paul sought out Ron Chase, the longtime director of a program called Sponsors, located in Lane County. The conversation was wide-ranging and lasted several hours. At the end of the conversation, Ron suggested that Paul apply for the case manager position that was closing that day. Shortly thereafter, in 2001, Ron Chase hired Paul.

Sponsors was founded in 1973 by a group of community activists and Catholic nuns. When Ron Chase took over as director in 1988, it was a small, fringe nonprofit. When Ron left, it had become an integral part of the public safety system in Lane County.

Paul reflects upon the man who hired him. "Ron was a Vietnam vet who grew up in New York, a self-described hippie. He had no real background for this work, but was a consummate activist."

Ron Chase realized that housing and employment were the cornerstones for success for people leaving the prison system. He created the agency's first transitional housing program in a house with five beds. By 2015, the agency operated 12 buildings on five sites with 145 beds.

Sponsors began to aggressively seek funding to support their work. They were hired to take on eight new contracts, in addition to the two existing ones. Then they launched a campaign to build a $6 million, 72-bed facility in the middle of the 2007-08 recession. Through a partnership with the Housing and Community Services Agency of Lane County, they began aggressively writing grants, seeking stimulus dollars, and tapping into funding from the Department of Veterans Affairs. "Ultimately, we were able to fund every dime of the $6 million construction cost," reflects Paul.

Ron was a significant mentor for Paul for 10 years, until Ron retired in 2011. He realized instinctively the challenge that nonprofits have in replacing charismatic founders like himself, and saw in Paul a person with potential for leadership. He began grooming Paul for leadership five years before he retired.

Paul is passionate about correcting the flaws in a criminal justice system which he has seen from both sides:

> *People in the prison system get a bus ticket back to their country of origin, a plastic bag with all their worldly possessions, and a pair of state-owned gray sweats. Most have no more than $20-$50 to their names. The fact that we still release people from prison to homelessness is at best short sighted and at worst extremely counterproductive. You don't have to have a bleeding heart to support the idea of getting people to the point where they can pay taxes and contribute.*

Paul reflects on his changed life:

> *It has taken me fifteen years to get a seat at the table. Now I have one. When I am in the public arena, I am selective about how I tell my story. I don't want people to make up their minds about me before they meet me. I made some*

mistakes many years ago, but that is not who I am. I don't want to be judged for the worst things I have ever done. It is easy to take people's criminal histories and label them for life. I would rather be judged for all I have done, good and bad.

It is very clear from Paul Solomon's work at Sponsors that the good far outweighs the bad. In 2015, Sponsors ran a mentoring program involving over 350 volunteers. The housing program served 350-400 people (over 3,000 since he started in 2001). Sponsors serves the highest-risk people. Most stay in the program for 3-4 months. They have a 65-70% success rate. To be deemed a success, clients must have passed all their drug and alcohol tests, found full time employment or schooling, complied with their parole conditions, and moved into permanent, sustainable housing. In 2015, Sponsors finished another capital campaign to complete a women's facility. Approximately two thirds of Lane County's prison population participates in Sponsors.

At the end of our interview, Paul reflects, "To know we have played some part in people's lives means a lot." As I walk out of Paul Solomon's small administrative office, I feel certain that Gus Solomon would be very proud of his grandson.

The Sister

"Customers can pay for their meal or they can work for it. Your work is as valuable as the change in your pocket. You keep your dignity."

Genny Nelson
February 2016

For all the stories in this book, I have avoided doing research until after the interview. This way, I can "discover" the interviewees at the same time that I learn about their lives and their work. So, when I set up an interview with the cofounder of Sisters Of The Road Cafe, Genny Nelson, I expected to meet a woman with a tough exterior and a big heart.

The woman who answers the door is not the person I expected. Genny welcomes me into her home with a soft voice and a gentle manner. Very early in the interview, she addresses the question that I never have to ask. "I grew up with middle-class habits in the working class."

Genny was born in Lewiston, Idaho and spent some of her early years with two older sisters and a younger brother in the middle-class suburbs of Medford, Oregon. Her father worked in forestry. When she was in fifth grade, her parents separated, and the children and their mother moved to inner city Medford.

A year later, her parents tried to work things out, and they moved to Portland, but the kids knew it wouldn't work. Their father left, this time for good. "Mom didn't have enough money. I saw people back then struggle to survive."

Growing up, Genny remembers feeling unworthy:

> *It affected my entire life, so, consequently, I have always worked on it. People would say hello to me, and I would respond by apologizing. I'm not proud of that. I discovered that you cannot love the world if you don't love yourself. I would often tell people at Sisters Of The Road that I brought my neuroses to the cafe.*

As she struggled with her sense of self, Genny was keenly aware of the world around her. She was raised Catholic and attended parochial schools from grade five through high school. She remembers asking her mother, "Why doesn't the Pope give the Church's riches to the poor?"

Genny always kept that question in her heart. It was clear to her that the world didn't treat all people equally, and that there was not "liberty and justice for all" in the United States. During her senior year in high school, she wrote a paper on Cesar Chavez and the grape boycott, interviewing not only workers and organizers, but also grocers and owners, so that she could get to the root of the problem.

A wake-up call early in life had given Genny a sense of urgency for acting on her values. In 1960, when she was just eight years old, she was diagnosed with type 1 diabetes. The doctors told her parents that she would not live beyond age 40. "I was in a race with my life. I had to accomplish in 20 years what would take most people 40."

The counterculture movements of the early '70s provided a backdrop for Genny to act on her values. The Vietnam war had been prolonged for more than a decade. The Black Panther Party and, later, the American Indian Movement, were shining a spotlight on the struggle for civil rights. Genny began attending Portland State University (PSU) in 1970 and paid for her tuition by participating in the federal work study program. In 1972 she started working at Burnside Projects Inc. This program was organized in 1969 by Fr. Gil Lulay, based in part on the values of the Catholic Worker Movement.

The Catholic Worker Movement was founded in 1933 by Dorothy Day and Peter Maurin. Genny describes it as "gentle personalism or nonviolent anarchism, involving no humiliation of anyone, including yourself, and the belief that standing up for each other's freedom is a personal responsibility."

> *I got the work study job in 1972, and it felt like coming home. I worked at the Everett Street Service Center, an all-night shelter, where I was surrounded by people who had chronic health problems—just like I did.*

The first evening on the job, Genny was very nervous. She received some advice from a coworker: "All you have to do is say hello and listen to people's stories and then tell your own."

The Service Center offered residents of the Burnside neighborhood a place to sleep, public restroom facilities, a mailing address, information and referral services, hotel outreach and advocacy, and most importantly, a place where people could come together socially. In 1972, in the fall of her junior year, Genny left PSU and accepted a full-time job with Burnside Projects Inc., as coordinator of volunteers.

In 1973, Genny married her first husband, who was a conscientious objector to the Vietnam War and involved with the local Catholic Worker Movement. Together in 1974, they opened a house of hospitality called Emmaus, where they lived with men, women and children who were referred to them by social service agencies, the police, and by each other on the street. Some stayed overnight and some stayed for a couple of years.

During their time at Emmaus House, she and her husband fostered and adopted their two children. After five years, her marriage ended, but she had found her life's work, and she began looking for another job. She got a job through the Comprehensive Employment and Training Act at Boxcar Bertha's.

Most Burnside neighborhood residents were men, but there were a growing number of women who, at the time, had nowhere to go. Boxcar Bertha's was a women-only center offering advocacy and support for women on the street. "It was a tiny place. We had a journal on the coffee table. Women could come in and talk or write about their calamities, surprises and little victories in their lives."

Sadly, the money for Boxcar Bertha's dried up. Genny and her coworker Sandy Gooch responded by visiting the area's missions and soup lines, asking the men and women they met about the unmet needs in their community. They discovered a huge gap in services provided, especially for women. The missions were only for men because they believed that women didn't belong on skid row. In addition, they required attendance at a religious service in exchange for a meal.

It was 1979, a time when many social service agencies were folding. Genny and Sandy were determined to go against the tide. "We wanted to create a place that would be lasting and safe for all, especially women and children—a place where they could barter their labor instead of their souls."

They opened Sisters Of The Road Cafe in Old Town Portland. Sandy brought the restaurant experience and Genny the philosophy. They wanted to offer job opportunities to people dealing with joblessness and homelessness every day. They recruited from their customers.

> We walked into a terrible recession and created our programs using philosophies of nonviolence and gentle personalism. I've always believed in praxis—reflection and action. We had all the action we could deal with, and sometimes didn't make time for reflection, resulting in mistakes.

Genny is very clear that Sisters was not a social service agency. "Customers can pay for their meal or they can work for it. Your work is as valuable as the change in your pocket. You keep your dignity."

Sisters Of The Road Cafe serves an average 225 meals a day for the cost of $1.50 per meal and beverage, a price that has changed little since inception. Those who cannot afford a meal can barter their labor in exchange for menu items at the Cafe. A customer can barter anywhere from 30 minutes to several hours, at the rate of six dollars per hour of meal credit.

According to Genny, "Customers tell us they don't want charity. They want to pay their own way, despite their low—or no—incomes. Sisters has always believed that you cannot do for people what they can do for themselves."

Sisters was established as a cooperative with a manager's collective. Membership in the cooperative with the right to create policy included attendance at all general meetings and a minimum of one two-hour work shift per week in the Cafe. Decisions were made by nonviolent consensus, and co-op members were accountable to each other.

Sisters has always been more than a restaurant. In the early years, Sisters designed a conflict resolution process that helped them walk their talk with customers and with each other. Genny reflects, "It takes a lot of energy and courage to practice nonviolence on a daily basis."

Sisters is locally involved with food justice issues and partners, believing that a just food system is important for community well-being. A just food system is accomplished by giving everyone access to food. In addition, Sisters is a regional and national ally, campaigning to pass a Homeless Bill of Rights in Oregon. Sisters has always said, "You have to go to the root of the problem before you can solve it. When you go to the root of homelessness, you uncover economic injustice."

In 2001, Genny provided the leadership and direction for an organizing project that involved one-to-one interviews with over five hundred men and women with experiences of homelessness. She contributed to both a manual about how to replicate this project and a book, published in 2007, that told the interviewees' stories, called *Voices from the Street: Truths about Homelessness from Sisters Of The Road*. Genny's work alongside people dealing with homelessness was recognized by the University of Portland, which awarded her an honorary doctorate in 2010.

In 2009 Genny retired due to health issues. In the summer of 2010, she suffered a heart attack. She has begun again to write and is heartened by the process. She visits Sisters from time to time for a meal or for an event. "I always feel welcome and experience Sisters' philosophies in action. Sisters is still profoundly about love."

Genny ends the interview with these thoughts:

> *In the last five years I have reflected a lot. Reflection is not always pretty and it can be harsh. But then there is forgiveness, and in forgiveness there is grace. I have a calmness in me that I am just beginning to feel. My job now is to share what I know with others. I will keep being the work.*

The Storyteller

"I believe in the power of words. My job has always been to help the community tell its story."

Trish Seiler
September 2015

Overflowing with art, jewelry and collectibles, Trish Seiler's 1900s-era home sits on a hill overlooking downtown Klamath Falls. In addition to raising her children in this home, Trish has lived here for over 36 years.

As I sit down at the dining room table after a tour, she gives me her business card, which says simply, "Trish Seiler, Storyteller." I ask her to tell me what that means, and she begins her story.

Trish was born in Mason City, Iowa, the fourth of eleven children. At the age of seven, her family moved to Sioux City, living in a large, four bedroom home with an attic for the boys' dorm. Having only one bathroom made getting ready for school a daily challenge.

Her mother was a farm girl who grew up on the "bottom road"

in Vermillion, South Dakota. Trish's father, also from Vermillion, lived about six blocks from the University of South Dakota. He joined the Air Force near the end of World War II, serving as a navigator on a bomber, and later served in the Korean War.

Trish contracted polio when she was three. She and two of her brothers were all sick at the same time, so her parents just assumed they all had the flu. But by the time her brothers recovered, Trish was unable to walk. Her parents took her to the hospital.

> *My earliest memories were of stark white hospital walls, an isolated room, and a door with a window, through which I could see my mother but could not touch her. It was 1954, the year the Salk vaccine came to our hometown—six months too late for me.*

After several months in the hospital, including some time in an iron lung, Trish was finally able to come home. She was wrapped in a blanket and placed on a couch in the front room. "I was unable to walk, but the first thing I did was wiggle out of the blanket, lower myself to the floor, and crawl to where my siblings were playing. I never looked back."

Her early life was difficult. Due to her father's position in the Air Force, the family moved often. Trish grew up with leg braces, many years before the Americans with Disabilities Act was enacted. In grade school, she climbed stairs, played on the playground, and walked from school to the church across the street for lunch. Still, she was often teased and bullied because she was "different."

When she was seven, Trish had surgery to help her walk and keep her balance. During the surgery, she was overdosed with anesthetics and was incapacitated for several days. This occurred again at age 20, when she had a heart attack on the surgery table and was placed in a medical coma for three days. Research has since shown that people with post-polio syndrome can only handle about half the normal amount of anesthetics.

Surviving made Trish a stronger, more responsible person.

> *Coming so close to death made me a tenacious person. When, at the age of nine, I was told by a doctor that I would never be able to have children, my five youngest siblings became my "bevy of quails."*

She smiles when telling a story about an incident when she was 14.

> *I took the younger kids trick-or-treating. An older and much bigger high school kid tried to steal candy from one of my brothers. I punched the guy in the face. He walked right into an uppercut to the chin. I really don't like bullies, in any form.*

Trish's troubles were not only outside the home. Her father was an alcoholic and could be violent in administering discipline to his kids. This led Trish to vow that if she had kids, they would always have a good place to come home to. It inspired her career working out of her home as the mother of two children.

After graduating from high school, Trish went on to receive her BA in social work at the University of South Dakota in

Vermillion. One of her earliest work experiences was in 1974 at the Pine Ridge Reservation in South Dakota, one year after it was occupied and taken over during the Wounded Knee incident. The reservation was one of the poorest communities in the country, with 50-65% unemployment. Alcoholism was one of the major causes of death.

She later went back to Vermillion and put her future husband through law school. They spent a year in Pierre, South Dakota, where he was clerk to the Chief Justice of the South Dakota Supreme Court.

When a family member from Eugene died, they moved to Oregon, where her husband got a job with Legal Aid in Klamath Falls and later in 1981 went into private practice.

From 1978 to 1980, Trish volunteered for the Hope-in-Crisis hotline. She became a VISTA worker in 1980, with the goal of establishing crisis centers in Klamath and Lake Counties, and became executive director of both crisis center programs. That same year, she helped obtain a federal grant to start a program for victims of domestic violence in Klamath Falls. The crisis line was expanded, and 24-7 rape crisis and suicide crisis teams were formed.

In 1985, Klamath Falls was rocked by three teen suicides. At the time, the focus of the community was on reaction, not prevention. Trish got involved; she wrote a successful grant that established youth prevention programs throughout the schools. As part of the program, she embarked on a speaking tour and visited all the schools. Trish explains:

Even though I was never trained as a grant writer, I am a good writer. I was trained as a counselor, but am also a good listener. I flunked debate in high school and never thought that I would get in front of people and talk about things that had happened in my life. But there was no one else to do it.

Her first speech to a civic organization was to 100 Rotarians, before women were allowed as members. According to Trish, "It was a success. Only four men walked out." Then she spoke to the all-female Soroptimists, where she was swarmed by women after her speech. Several years later, they presented her with the Women Helping Women award, based on her work with domestic violence.

In 1986 Trish realized that her two children needed a more stable home life. She stepped down from her position at the crisis center, but did not retire from civic life. "I figured I could raise my kids, raise money, and raise hell at the same time. So I founded my business, Seiler Consultants, to assist the nonprofit sector in board development, fundraising and grant writing."

Her business was operated out of her home. At the same time, she started volunteering on boards and commissions dealing with families and children, as well as serving two terms on the Klamath Falls City School Board. She also served on the Klamath Falls Community College Board and the Klamath Falls City Council.

The list of organizations Trish has served in the capacity of fundraising, board development and strategic planning is lengthy. Her contributions range from securing a $600,000 grant for the Veterans Memorial Park expansion and raising support for the Klamath Falls Skatepark to working with supporters of the Klamath Basin Restoration Agreement and helping several other community organizations come together to raise $4 million to address the needs of the region's children.

Among her favorite projects was raising funds for handicapped-accessible playground equipment for Conger School. It was not a big-money project, but it was especially meaningful for Trish, given her childhood disability. Trish recalls that day:

> *They wanted new playground equipment for the school. A challenge they faced was that the classroom for developmentally delayed kids was on the opposite side of the building from the playing field. I convinced the school to knock a hole in the wall and create a ramp to the playground, giving the special needs kids access to ADA equipment. The construction of the ramp cost $10,000, but it was all donated by the community. The actual playground structure was paid for with a $30,000 grant from Meyer Memorial Trust. During the ceremony to celebrate the new playground, a 7-year-old child in a wheelchair demonstrated the use of the new equipment. You couldn't hold him back!*

Trish reflects on the 30 years since she "retired" as an executive director and started her business of supporting nonprofit and community-based projects.

> *I believe in the power of words. My job has always been to help the community tell its story. Every nonprofit has a job to do: to tell their story in such a way that the community will see themselves in it, and thus support the organization.*

Although Trish spent only the first few years of her career leading a nonprofit organization, she has left her mark on many nonprofits over the past three decades. Her gift as a storyteller has helped her community strengthen elected boards, increase access to higher education, improve parks, and promote tourism and economic development. But for all that she has done, she remains humble about her achievements. "Most people don't know the projects I have done because my name is not on the rooms or buildings. I research and write the grant applications, but my clients sign them."

Trish Seiler's dedication to championing the underdog has made her community a safer place for victims of domestic violence and sexual assault, people with disabilities, and troubled youth. She overcame a difficult childhood, including a volatile home life and a severe physical handicap, to become an influential, if unsung, leader in her community.

The Rebel

"I see myself as a communitarian, responsible for making my corner of the world better. There is a sacredness in all of us. I see it in most people."

Michael Eichman
July 2010

Michael Eichman grew up the oldest of six boys on a low-income family farm in eastern Colorado. The dryland farm had been in the family for several generations. Michael's father, who was from the first generation of his family to speak English, had grown up there, too. He had been raised by his older brother, as both of their parents were deceased. The strict German disciplinarian approach with which he raised Michael was the best way he knew to prepare Michael to succeed in a tough world.

Michael reflects on his childhood, "I was a challenge—rebellious, undisciplined, and very stubborn. I couldn't believe that my father knew anything about my world and where I was going. I wasn't ready to listen."

Among the most vivid memories of Michael's childhood was

the time in fifth grade when he learned about Adolf Eichmann. The association of his last name with a Nazi war criminal had a powerful influence on him. He became aware of the presence of evil in the world. At the same time, he began to develop a strong commitment to being a force for good.

In junior high school, Michael had his first experience with an adult mentor. His gym teacher, Ray Luntz, organized youths to help children with disabilities participate in sports and other recreational activities. Michael resonated with this activity, which met his needs to be useful and to have a purpose.

He continued to pursue services for people with disabilities through the Colorado Association for Retarded Citizens (ARC), and he encouraged his friends to join him. He started organizing recreational activities for summer camps and, at age 16, Michael became president of the Colorado Youth ARC.

For Michael, academics took a backseat to his community work. He credits his mother with getting him through high school. Unlike his father, who dropped out of school after tenth grade, Michael's mother achieved her goal, graduating from high school in May after marrying Michael's father in April. Her belief in the importance of a high school diploma might have been the only thing that kept Michael in school.

After graduation, Michael saw that his future lay far beyond the plains of eastern Colorado. He ventured out alone, with little but a backpack and the clothes on his back, hopping freight trains heading west.

He arrived in Oregon at age 19. A three-week Outward Bound

program during that first year in Oregon reinforced his belief in himself as a leader. Inspired by his Outward Bound experience, Michael became one of three founders of a nonprofit summer camp located on the Little North Fork of the Santiam River.

Also in his first year in Oregon, Michael received a Stafford Loan to attended Oregon College of Education (OCE) in Monmouth. At OCE he began as a work-study student with Teaching Research, a program respected for its innovative work in special education. Michael worked on campus as a classroom aide for children with disabilities. His involvement with Teaching Research continued, and he worked with a group home for children with disabilities as part of a national research project. The distractions of community service caused him to drop out of school, a year short of receiving his BA.

Later, Michael was hired by Head Start in Salem, serving for five years as a Family Advocate. The position was based upon the assumption that the only way to successfully educate low-income and disadvantaged young children is to involve the whole family. He liked his new job, but his concerns with the overall leadership of the program encouraged him to leave Head Start and return to OCE. At OCE he achieved a lifelong goal of being the first person in his family to attain a college degree.

After completing his degree in education and being recognized as one of the four outstanding graduates of his OCE class, Michael was hired to teach fifth grade in Yamhill County. But he would again become frustrated with his role. The education system, with its bureaucracy and rules, was a shock to Michael, and he left teaching after one year.

Head Start again recruited Michael, who reluctantly agreed to an administrative role, supervising Family Advocates. In this new role, Michael was confronted with a system of performance standards that smelled of the same bureaucracy that had driven him out of K-12 teaching. But being more seasoned, he decided to work with the rules—and around them—as necessary.

"I was a rebel. But I decided to quit battling the system and learn what the performance standards were and how to use them to the benefit of kids and families."

In 1995, armed with a vision of how to be innovative and at the same time to work within the regulations, Michael applied and was accepted to be the director of Yamhill County Head Start.

Entering this new role with lofty expectations, Michael encountered immediate challenges. The Head Start agency, operated by Yamhill County, had only $17,000 in the bank. Michael's predecessor had embezzled over $350,000. The county sheriff, who served as chair of the board, told Michael not to tell the Head Start regional office. Michael shunned his advice and put his cards on the table. Head Start was removed from the administrative control of Yamhill County, and Michael worked with the community to establish a separate nonprofit organization, Friends of Head Start, which took over the original program.

In establishing the board of the new organization, Michael turned to the very people who benefited from the program to take on lead roles. Many of these people responded to Michael's trust and respect by being outstanding leaders.

The key for me was to respect these people. They can be rough and uneducated. They lack sophistication, but they want power. They remind me of myself growing up in a low-income family in eastern Colorado.

Over time, the Yamhill Head Start program established a culture of learning, which respected children and their families. Starting with fewer than one hundred students in 1995, the number of students in the program grew to over 170 in 1997 and over 350 in 2010. With the help of grants, private funding and major gifts of land, Michael led the effort to build or repurpose new Head Start buildings in Newberg, Sheridan, and Dayton. The buildings were all designed and built with energy efficiency and sustainability in mind.

When Michael talks about the source of his inspiration, he reflects, "We are all called—guided by a higher power—to make the world a better place. People get too rooted in the rules of faith, not in the call to share our humanity."

In 2012, the community of McMinnville dedicated its new, repurposed Head Start building and named it the Michael Eichman Center, just at the time when Michael had been diagnosed with ALS. Shortly after the dedication, he had to step down from the leadership of the organization that he so dearly loved.

As Michael struggled through the unrelenting assault of ALS, he took great satisfaction that his leadership had touched the lives of hundreds of children and families in Yamhill County, Oregon. Michael Eichman was a rebel who found his purpose and became a force for good in the world.

Author's note: Michael Eichman passed away in the fall of 2014. He died on his own terms, taking advantage of Oregon's death with dignity statute, surrounded by loving friends and family.

III

Collaboration

Jordan, Pippen and Rodman; Lennon and McCartney; Helen Keller and Anne Sullivan—throughout history, teamwork and the sharing of vision and ideas have led to outstanding achievements. For the five people featured in this chapter, the act of reaching out to others and working together to solve important societal problems was more than a means to an end—it was the key to their success.

The Scientist
Research scientist **Dr. Kent Thornburg** had a chance encounter with a pediatric cardiac surgeon whose office was just down the hall. Their brief conversation about a surgery to be performed on a baby that very day not only may have saved a life—it also changed the course of Kent's life.

The Lightning Rod
When a Salem political leader lamented the lack of involvement of churches in Salem's growing problem with gang violence, it opened a door for **Sam Skillern**, who was searching for work where his faith and his vocation could come together.

The Elder
Terry Cross moved to Portland in 1978, just three months before the Indian Child Welfare Act empowered Oregon's 46 tribes to run their own child welfare programs. Over the next 16 years, he worked tirelessly to unify tribes at the state, Northwest, and ultimately, the national level.

The Dreamer
Acting on his belief that schools alone cannot meet society's high aspirations for today's students, **Mark Langseth** serves the most challenging schools—not by providing direct service, but by bringing in other organizations to serve as partners in student success.

The Community Builder
Kelly Poe is among eastern Oregon's most respected nonprofit leaders. Although she has never led a nonprofit organization herself, her passion for solving community problems has inspired others.

The Scientist

"Scientists who work across political boundaries can bring new insights to disease that could never be discovered alone."

Dr. Kent Thornburg
July 2010

In 1992, Dr. Kent Thornburg was living a dream. A self-proclaimed "science addict" all his life, he was in his second decade working as a teacher and research scientist at Oregon Health and Science University (OHSU). But an event occurred that year which changed the course of his life. The head pediatric cardiac surgeon at OHSU, Dr. Adnan Cobanoglu, was talking with Kent about a surgery he was getting ready to perform on a baby with pulmonary artery constriction.

Cobanoglu lamented, "I wish I knew what effect the constriction had on the muscles of the ventricles."

"You should talk with me," Kent replied. "I've been studying this for twenty years!"

Dr. Cobanoglu, whose office was very near to Kent's, laughed,

"This shouldn't be happening at OHSU."

A light went on for Kent. "At that moment we decided that we lived in isolated worlds. The discovery was a driving force for me."

Kent Thornburg grew up on a small farm in rural Oregon. His father taught fifth grade and managed the farm. Lovers of science, his parents were thrilled that young Kent was showing interest at a very early age. For his tenth birthday they gave him a chemistry kit.

His sixth grade teacher, Roland Kerr, further encouraged Kent by showing him how little he really knew. "He provided the right kind of stimulation to make you dissatisfied with where you were."

Kent went on to study as an undergraduate at George Fox College, with the goal of becoming a doctor. One of his professors, Elver Voth, discouraged him. "Kent, you don't want to be a doctor. You should aspire to go into medical research. Go to Oregon State University and get your Ph.D." Kent reflects:

> *My interest in practicing medicine faded away. Doctors don't have the opportunity to sit on the edge of their chairs and wonder what causes the diseases they treat. I discovered in graduate school that I was addicted to science.*

As a doctoral student at OSU, Kent was mentored by Howard Hilleman, a linguist and a scientist. Hilleman helped Kent understand the importance of language and writing in order to make science accessible to the lay audience. Kent carried that knowledge forward into his career, where his ability to capture the imagination of individuals ranging from donors to scientist peers has enhanced both his reputation and funding for his work.

After receiving his Ph.D, Kent spent a brief time at Washington University in St. Louis before moving to OHSU in 1973 to serve as a physiology teacher and researcher.

It was nearly two decades later, in 1992, when Kent had that fateful exchange with Dr. Cobanoglu in the hallway. Following that chance meeting, the two agreed to collaborate. Kent set off to recruit colleagues with a passion for cardiac research. Working with Dr. Cobanoglu, he brought both clinical cardiologists and cardiovascular researchers together, allowing them to combine their knowledge and expertise toward a clinical application. They asked five different departments to help out, securing $5,000 from each to support this cross-departmental collaboration.

It was during this recruitment and organizational process that Kent's vision for teamwork in science took root. He attracted his colleagues with a powerful message: "Scientists who work across political boundaries can bring new insights to disease that could never be discovered alone."

In 1993, Kent was the driving force behind the creation of the Heart Research Center at OHSU. It was built on a philosophy very different from the one that dominated scientific research at the time, which was: "Hire the best people and let them compete by themselves for space and money." Instead, it encouraged outstanding new hires to work in teams and help each other succeed.

Over the last two decades, this concept has taken hold at OHSU. Many people were aware that politics and the "silo-like environment" in scientific research were problems. The collaborative research approach was a welcome change. At the same time, the OHSU Cancer Institute was just being formed, based on the same collaborative philosophy. Kent reflects:

> *I don't take credit for these developments. A lot of people were thinking this way; but I am proud of the fact that the Heart Research Center brought these people together. There are more success stories than I can tell here.*

Collaboration on the hill was not enough for Kent. Over time, he was becoming dissatisfied with the job scientists were doing in communicating their work to the community at large. "I admit to being incompetent in the community. I don't have the training to bring medical knowledge to the community." But he had the vision, as well as the gift instilled by Howard Hilleman and cultivated throughout his career to communicate complex, technical concepts into language that the lay public could understand.

Kent was driven to make the Heart Research Center more socially responsible and to bring world-class expertise in the developmental origins of health and disease to Oregon. To achieve these ends, he recruited Dr. David Barker from the UK to collaborate with the center. David shared Kent's commitment to social responsibility.

David Barker's UK research findings linking maternal nutrition to the lifelong health of babies became a driving force behind the Center's outreach to the community. By 2012, the Heart Research Center was spawning over $40 million in grants and departmental support per year. Kent's challenge was to continue his own research, reach out to the community, and, at the same time, do the management work required to "feed the beast." He survived based on a leadership style of "finding talented people, encouraging their great ideas, and helping them find what they need to be successful." He adds, "They don't need to be in my department. I am not political."

In 2011, Bob Moore, founder of Bob's Red Mill, was inspired to donate $25 million to OHSU. This gift resulted in the creation of the Bob and Charlee Moore Institute for Nutrition and Wellness, whose mission is to bring research on maternal nutrition to bear on society through education and outreach. In addition to running his lab and the Heart Research Center, Kent was asked to be director of the Institute in January 2012.

A year after the Moore gift, in 2012, Phil and Penny Knight gave $125 million to OHSU to fund cardiovascular research and treatment. Kent credits Dr. Albert Starr and Dr. Sanjiv Kaul as the key players who worked with the Knights in planning the gift.

Shortly after the gift announcement, OHSU hosted a large gathering to celebrate and announce the new opportunities brought on by the Knight gift. At that meeting, Albert Starr described how Phil Knight's eyes would light up when Kent talked about the power of breaking down the academic silos, linking scientific research to clinical practice, and taking scientific knowledge directly to the community, where it can influence public health.

The Knights' gift was inspired by these discussions. The gift came with the stipulation that the clinical and research arms of OHSU's new Knight Cardiovascular Institute be housed together to promote the application of scientific research directly to the health of the community. The Heart Research Center was placed underneath the Knight Cardiovascular Institute and became the Center for Developmental Health. Its purpose is to investigate the reasons why poor nutrition before birth leads to disease later in life.

Successful funding has driven Kent Thornburg to work tirelessly to achieve his vision. He has launched a statewide nutrition consortium, aimed at educating low-income, food-challenged Oregonians on the importance of good nutrition and strategies for improving nutrition on a low budget. He is also working with leaders of the Latino health community to reverse the trend toward obesity and chronic disease among the children and grandchildren of Oregon's Latino immigrants.

In 2013, Kent lost his longtime scientific partner and friend David Barker. He is now keeping up with his own workload while fulfilling his and Barker's commitments and obligations nationally and internationally.

As successful as he has been, Kent is driven to move forward, remembering the advice of his sixth grade teacher Roland Kerr—to always be dissatisfied with where you are. So Kent remains on the edge of his chair, eyes and heart open to the challenges that lie ahead.

The Lightning Rod

> "Two hundred churches in Salem all used to be cocoons, only used on Wednesday nights and Sunday mornings. What a waste!"
>
> Sam Skillern
> June 2015

My interview with Sam Skillern takes place at the Ike Box Coffee Shop, a repurposed former funeral home in Salem, Oregon, which is one of the projects supported by the Salem Leadership Foundation (SLF).

During the two hours I spend with Sam, people keep coming up to him and visiting—a coffee shop employee who is involved in an SLF project, two young kids who show their artwork to Sam, and a rabbi who talks with Sam about an upcoming event at the synagogue. I tell Sam not to apologize. These "distractions" are part of his story. And Sam is a storyteller!

Sam's parents met at the University of Oregon. After college, they married and moved to Salem, where Sam's father got started in the insurance business. Sam grew up in Salem, a name which he delights in telling me was derived from the

Hebrew word "shalom" or "peace and well-being."

As a boy, Sam wore a brace on his left ankle to straighten his malformed leg. "Fourth grade was very tough. I was made fun of because of my disability. But a fellow fourth-grader, Jim Goodwin, took me under his wing and encouraged me to play baseball."

From fourth grade to community college, baseball played a very significant role in Sam's life. Sam refers to baseball as his "confidence factor." He had leg surgery in sixth grade and then went on to play middle school varsity in seventh grade and became an all star at the high school and community college levels. "Because of my leg, I always had humility. Because of Jim and his parents, I had confidence."

During this time, Sam's faith journey was solidified through his involvement with St. Paul's Episcopal Church and Young Life camps.

After graduating from high school, Sam attended Oregon State University (OSU). "I crammed four years into five," he quipped. Failing to find a spiritual home, Sam just partied. "I don't recommend it, but I did it." He began as a business major. It seemed logical to him, as he ran a painting business in high school and in college, and entrepreneurism was always a part of his life. The coursework he loved, however, was not business but writing and poetry; he ended up majoring in journalism with a minor in business.

In 1982, in the middle of a huge economic downturn in the Northwest, Sam graduated from OSU. He moved to Seattle in search of a journalism or public relations job, and it took him a year to find one. Seattle Goodwill paid him $4.19 per hour for doing press releases and an employee newsletter. Despite the low pay, Sam calls it "one of the best jobs I've ever had."

He left Goodwill after 16 months and took a job with Arst Public Relations in Seattle, where he worked from 1984 to 1993. Sam remembers:

> *Working with Jane Arst was great. We were different. I was a young Christian guy from a state university. She was a wise Jewish progressive who was magna cum laude from Wellesley College. At first she intimidated me, but I grew to deeply admire her. She was a glass ceiling breaker and taught me a ton about business and life.*

Sam had clients across the disciplines—health care, municipalities, nonprofits, real estate, and education. Some of his favorite work was for pro bono clients. He was a "neighborhood advocate" for Habitat for Humanity, focusing on getting land donated for building projects and then helping the surrounding neighbors accept the Habitat family. Through this project, he began to see how his faith and his vocation could work together.

After Jane left Arst Public Relations, Sam continued to get contracts with other organizations, but none would hire him for full-time ministry work, which was what he felt called to do.

During this time, a Young Life friend from high school, Martin Barrett, came to recruit Sam to come back to Salem. Martin was a founding board member of the Salem Leadership Foundation. They had a board, but no staff, and were interested in Sam because of his experience with so many different organizations and projects. Initially, Sam said no, but he and his wife decided to pray about it. It soon became clear to Sam what he needed to do: "My call to ministry turned out to be back in my home town of Salem."

The SLF job did not come easily. Sam traveled to Salem for four interviews. The board was cautious; Sam did not have a divinity degree or pastoral experience. The process went on for nearly a year. When Sam finally got the job offer, he and his wife chose to accept it. What attracted Sam to the job was that it combined church and community.

The roots of SLF were formed in the early 1990s. At that time, a local newspaper headline read, "Youth Gangs Plague City." Representative Peter Courtney formed a Gang Intervention Task Force. He wanted top leadership from the community to get involved, and became upset when no clergy were recruited to participate.

The response from his colleagues to this concern was, "Why would we want them? Gangs are a social problem, not a spiritual one." Courtney, a Catholic, insisted by responding, "Go find me some clergy. If we don't have churches involved, this won't work." Special invitations were sent out to clergy. Many did not respond. For those who did get involved, it became a huge time commitment, and attendance dropped.

Dick Lucco, senior pastor from Trinity Covenant Church, was unwilling to give up. Under his leadership, a team of church, business and civic leaders looked at other Christian community development models around the country. Ray Bakke from Chicago was invited to visit Salem. He helped Rev. Lucco and others to establish the Salem Leadership Foundation in early 1996.

Sam describes the SLF philosophy:

> *We embrace and live out what we believe, but we don't push it either. That way, a very diverse group of people can work together on a common cause. Jane Arst taught me that true compromise—finding the highest and best outcome for the most parties—is an elegant thing.*

The SLF model is unique in that it does not directly run programs. According to Sam, "Our board realizes that there are already so many nonprofits. We don't need to start our own programs, but support programs that are already doing great work to lead and serve."

A fundamental element of the SLF is Churches as Neighborhood (CaN) Centers. Sam describes the philosophical underpinnings of the CaN Centers:

> *Two hundred churches in Salem all used to be cocoons, only used Wednesday nights and Sunday mornings. What a waste! Our role is to call churches to serve others ... from cocoon to community catalyst.*

For seven years, the SLF had been calling suburban churches into the inner city. Recently the focus changed, and the emphasis was placed upon each church doing ministry in its own community. Sam stresses that there is poverty there too, "not only material poverty, but the poverty of affluence."

Currently there are 21 official CaN Centers and 25-30 congregations that are in the process of becoming CaN Centers. Becoming a CaN Center involves a three-year training process and a commitment to raising funds to support local programs, typically run through the auspices of local partner organizations. According to Sam, "140 local congregations still don't want to mix."

SLF has 10 staff members (7.25 full-time equivalent) and a budget of approximately $630,000. The goal is to have one staff person known as a "Lightning Rod" in each high school feeder area. Sam is the Lightning Rod for the North Salem area, in addition to being executive director.

When I ask Sam to tell me about the major achievements of SLF, he talks about some of the projects in which SLF has participated with local partners. At Hope Station, developed by First Church of the Nazarene, low-income families pay $30 per month and volunteer their time in exchange for $200 in food, clothing and household items.

The Northwest Hub was founded by Evergreen Presbyterian's outreach pastor and former bicycle shop worker, Kirk Seyfert. Homeless adults and youths "earn a bike" by volunteering 10-15 hours on bike repair and out in the community. One year and 300 bikes later, Kirk and his team are opening the Northwest Hub Cycling Shop.

Sam could have told similar stories all day! He is modest about his leadership style. "I'm a great storyteller, but not a great closer; a great modeler, but not a great manager."

Sam's high energy and all-consuming commitment to his work and community are not without cost. He and the Salem Leadership Foundation have not chosen an easy mission. When the early founders of SLF were advised that "gangs are a social problem, not a spiritual one," they saw first hand the difficulty of getting churches to look beyond their walls and into the community. Over the ministry's 21 years, the good times and difficult times, Sam and his family and team have weathered the challenges with faith and joy.

Despite the challenges, more than 60 churches in Salem, Oregon are reaching out with love to their neighborhoods and working together to coordinate efforts and increase their impact. The one factor that has made Salem successful where so many communities have failed is a tireless crusader whose enthusiasm, raw energy and abundance of optimism have shown the people of Salem that it can work. Congratulations, Sam Skillern, and Godspeed as you continue your ministry!

The Elder

> "In tribal culture, esteem and identity come from service. You sit down and listen to the elders. You are a servant. The elders are up front. Then, suddenly, they call upon you to step up and do it."
>
> Terry Cross
> July 2012

Terry Cross, a member of the Seneca Nation, was born in western New York and raised near the town of Cassadaga. He grew up in a poor family on a dairy farm, just off the reservation. His father was white and his mother Seneca.

"We didn't know we were poor. If you worked hard, you could eat. Our mother said we were rich in family and friends."

His father had a very strong work ethic and became a justice of the peace. His mother's heritage valued the importance of family and service. She would tell Terry, "You don't turn people down when they need help."

Growing up, Terry spent a lot of time with his maternal grandparents on the Allegheny Reservation, south of Buffalo, New York. He couldn't read until the fourth grade. He was labeled "slow and sullen." His mother was told that "Indians can't read."

It turned out that Terry had a vision problem. He barely made it through grade school. But in high school he began to excel, and, with the support of the Seneca National Education Foundation, he attended Grove City College in Pennsylvania. The Foundation was established with funds derived from a legal settlement as a result of the construction of the Kinzua Dam, which caused a flood that washed away tribal land.

Initially, Terry's ambition was to become an attorney, but his focus changed as a result of a field placement working with youths at a reform school in inner-city Philadelphia. "That experience put the fire of social justice in me. Sociology and social work became my niche."

After graduating cum laude from Grove City College, Terry became a case aide, assisting child welfare caseworkers for Mercer County, Pennsylvania. Upon graduation, he passed the civil service exam and became a caseworker, and at 21 was knocking on doors, investigating child abuse and neglect. His supervisor at Mercer County saw his potential and encouraged him to pursue a scholarship, which enabled Terry to attend Portland State University (PSU), where he received a Master in Social Work degree.

According to Terry, "At PSU, I participated in an Indian Education Project and claimed my 'Indianness.'"

After graduate school, Terry went back to the Allegheny Reservation to work as a school social worker. He remembers:

> *These were the best and the worst years of my life. I was young and idealistic and came under huge pressure from both sides. Some Indians saw me as a sellout with a white man's education. The non-Indian administrators didn't want me to succeed. After all, they were making money off "the Indian problem."*

As he confronted the racism of the teachers and administrative staff, the superintendent told Terry to stop. He was the victim of character assassination, and his life was threatened.

Terry modestly describes the secret for his success in battling this adversity as "showing up." Throughout that difficult time, the tribal elders served as both his teachers and protectors. Terry explains:

> *In tribal culture, esteem and identity come from service. I came to work because there was a need. I would sit down and listen to the elders. The elders were always up front. I saw myself as a servant. The elders taught me. Then suddenly they would say, "You are speaking today."*

In June of 1978, Terry moved back to Portland, where he was hired by the Parry Center. "I knew I needed credentials. I got them at the Parry Center."

In September 1978, Congress passed the Indian Child Welfare Act. The act empowered tribes to run their own child welfare programs. According to Terry, "At the time, there were only about a hundred Indians with MSWs in the US, and fewer than twelve of them were in child welfare."

Collaboration

Terry started getting called to do workshops. By the fall of 1982, he was using all of his vacation time training child welfare workers across the Pacific Northwest, as well as teaching at PSU. The State of Oregon wanted to buy three weeks of his time, so they contacted the Parry Center.

The Parry Center's response was, "This sounds important. How can we help you?" Terry was impressed by the Parry Center's ability to look beyond its own programs and see the value of collaboration. Ross Miller at the Parry Center was a great mentor. He told Terry, "Write a proposal. Dream!"

Terry's reaction: "You could have knocked me over with a feather."

At the time, there were 46 recognized tribes in Oregon, Washington, and Idaho; but only 17 had started child welfare programs. Terry consulted with the tribes and convinced them that they all would be stronger if they worked together. The tribes proposed to funders that the Northwest Indian Child Welfare Institute be created. 11 months later, they opened their doors, with the help of a grant from the Northwest Area Foundation and financial support from the Parry Center.

Terry worked with the 17 tribes to develop a culturally specific training curriculum using Indian trainers, and put together a collaborative network of the programs then in operation. In the first two years, they trained 14 trainers and developed 11 training manuals. At that time they asked the Parry Center for continued support and received two more years of funding.

After the four-year incubation period, Terry convened 50

tribal child welfare directors and elders to develop a culturally sensitive plan. They explored whether to join the Affiliated Tribes of Northwest Indians; instead, in 1987, they established a stand-alone organization, the Northwest Indian Child Welfare Association. In 1989, the organization expanded into California and Montana; in 1994, it took on a national focus and became the National Indian Child Welfare Association (NICWA).

The NICWA board is made up of tribal leaders, child welfare professionals, and others representing various business fields. It receives approximately equal funding through fees for service, foundation grants, and federal contracts. Terry refuses to seek funds from the Bureau of Indian Affairs or the Indian Health Service, as he feels these funds are needed in communities. "We only seek grants or contracts that do not compete with tribes for scarce resources."

Since 1987, the NICWA has made a major difference, completing over 100 funded projects, grants and contracts, with budgets ranging in size from $5,000 to $5 million. Since its inception, NICWA's advocacy has brought more than $3 billion to Indian tribes and organizations, expanding access to many federal programs to which tribes had no previous access, including child care, temporary assistance to needy families, foster care, child abuse prevention, and children's mental health.

In 2015, Terry Cross stepped down as executive director of NICWA, following a four-year succession plan. After spending over 30 years bringing together diverse tribes from around the country to create a unified approach to Indian child welfare,

Terry sensed that the time was right for change. "As a founding director, I knew that the most important thing I could do was to successfully transition the leadership of NICWA to the next generation."

Although he has stepped aside as director, Terry has no intention of retiring any time soon. He is devoting his time to hands-on projects in tribal communities, teaching and mentoring younger staff, and is in the process of writing about his experience. He has fully embraced his new role as an elder, in his words, "helping to inform the next generation of emerging community-change agents in Indian Country."

The Dreamer

> "If we think that schools in poverty-impacted communities can do it alone, it is insanity."
>
> Mark Langseth
> March 2013

Since its founding in 1990, "I Have a Dream" Oregon had been very successful in adopting entire third grade classes in low-income schools and following the students all the way through college. But when I sit down to interview President and CEO Mark Langseth in March of 2013, Mark says he is not satisfied with the successes of the past; and a recent development has him on the edge of his seat. "I Have a Dream" Oregon has identified an entire school that understands that they alone cannot be successful in transforming student outcomes. They need the help of serious community partners working alongside school personnel and families in order to change students' lives for the better.

Mark Langseth grew up in a small town in Minnesota, whose population of 1,600 included 600 inmates who resided in the local correctional facility. His father was a dentist, but that wasn't his passion. He was also an artist, sculptor and small business entrepreneur.

His mother was a dental hygienist who took up writing and went on to become the editor of the local newspaper. Both parents had a strong sense of social justice. His father was the only dentist in town who treated Native Americans, and his mother was involved in countless community projects. The family philosophy was: "Do the right thing in the community."

Growing up, Mark appreciated the "We're all in this together" nature of the small town, but knew that small town living was not for him. He remembers saying to himself at the age of five, "Get me into a city!"

College provided the ticket to the big city, as Mark attended the University of Minnesota. Involvement with the University YMCA turned him on to community work, and the National Youth Leadership Council was his first "class" as a lifelong student of leadership. According to Mark, "Leadership is the inability to sit by and watch the world go to hell."

After graduating in 1985, Mark founded the first statewide campus service-learning initiative in the nation, which he later transitioned into the Minnesota Campus Compact, a coalition of over 40 college and university presidents committed to the civic purposes of higher education. Throughout the process he discovered that "real change is possible."

Working with the National Youth Leadership Council, Mark also had the opportunity to ally with Democratic Senator Ted Kennedy and Republican Senator David Durenberger with the message that young people from his generation were truly interested in serving their communities. This discussion ultimately led to federal legislation establishing Americorps and related national service programs.

Later in his career, Mark was involved in higher education administration and fundraising. Although he enjoyed the work, "It was a detour." When his daughter's best friend was killed in an auto accident, "it jolted me back to what I'm passionate about—equity for kids who have not had equitable access to educational success."

Mark was hired by "I Have a Dream" Oregon in 2009. He expresses pride in the fact that they have worked with over 900 students since 1990, providing mentoring, academic and social support and creating a college/career culture. In 2012 and 2013, 90% of the students who were served graduated from high school, and 70% went on to postsecondary education.

In spite of these successes, both Mark and his board were not satisfied, because they felt the program still did not sufficiently impact education systems or the larger community. As a result, they envisioned a new initiative—to partner with an entire low-income school and go beyond the role of direct service provider, instead mobilizing other service providers to join in a transformative, collaborative, long-term effort.

Mark's excitement on the day of the interview is based on "I Have a Dream" Oregon's recent adoption of the entire Alder Elementary School, a K-5 school of 500 students in the Reynolds School District, where over 95% of students receive free/reduced-price lunches, over 85% of students are students of color, and where over 20 languages are spoken.

"I Have a Dream" Oregon had just developed a 15-year contract with the Reynolds School District and called upon other service providers to join the effort to transform college and career results for students who begin their academic journey at Alder.

And they did—over 40 partner organizations included colleges and universities, as well as leading nonprofits such as Friends of the Children, SMART, Home Forward and Human Solutions.

One of the six practices of high-performing nonprofits identified in *Forces for Good* (by Leslie Crutchfield and Heather McLeod Grant) is to treat other nonprofits as allies, not competitors for scarce resources. The "I Have a Dream" strategic partnership approach exemplifies that strategy.

One of the most powerful concepts behind the Dreamer School model is that the community ought to take primary responsibility for helping reduce poverty related student and family barriers that inhibit student learning, thereby enabling schools to focus on teaching and learning.

According to Mark:

> *We spot the great organizations, bring them together around a vision, and just hope when we build it, they will come. One thing I look for in people is inspiration around vision. They have to believe. The bar is high. We cannot afford anything less than absolute alignment if we want success.*

Mark Langseth and "I Have a Dream" Oregon have truly set the bar high in inspiring kids and families to assume that college is in their future. With Mark's passion for educational equity and the help of others, they will surely succeed!

The Community Builder

> "One of the challenges I have is that people think I am supporting projects that were my ideas. That's rarely the case. I'm good at listening and supporting other people's good ideas."
>
> Kelly Poe
> November 2015

As I was planning a trip to eastern Oregon to interview nonprofit leaders, the name that most frequently came up when I asked for nominees was Kelly Poe. I looked her up online and saw that she was currently an employee of the Malheur Education Service District. Going back further in her career, I learned she had been Director of the Malheur County Commission on Children and Families. I scratched my head; both of these organizations are arms of local government—not private nonprofits.

My curiosity was aroused, so I called Kelly. She was the only person I talked with who said that she was a bad choice for an interview … not because she was not a nonprofit leader, but because her story was not interesting. Now I was intrigued—enough to drive to Ontario, Oregon, a small town on the Idaho border, for a cup of coffee and a visit with Kelly.

Kelly was born in Boise, Idaho, the youngest of four kids. Her mother had lost her father when she was eight. At that point, in 1943, Kelly's mother's family sold the farm and moved into town. They were very poor. Even though her mother had a successful career in management for US Bank, she always held tightly to the secret that she never finished high school.

Kelly's father married her mother when they were both very young. Later, the family moved to Payette, Idaho, where he worked with the Idaho State Police for 20 years.

According to Kelly:

> *He was a peace officer, not a police officer. He approached every vehicle assuming that the driver was a good person who had simply made a mistake. For my dad, all people were good. My family never classified people, whether by class, race or poverty.*

In eighth grade, Kelly's life was disrupted when her father left home to start a new life. There was no family support to help her attend college. Instead, she met a young man from Fruitland, Idaho, whom she married when she graduated from high school. Her husband worked as a plumber, and Kelly credits a high school business teacher for giving her the office skills she needed to get a job. At age 21, they had a daughter, and a year later they moved to Portland, where they had a son when Kelly was 24. At age 27, Kelly and her family moved to Seattle.

Kelly became involved in her children's private school, where she served as a volunteer substitute teacher and a leader of community efforts to support the school. The teachers gave her a lot of positive feedback about the work she was doing with kids. She particularly loved overseeing kids on the playground, remembering that it was the playground, as much as the classroom, that had shaped her identity when she was in school. She was also part of a team that built a volunteer child care program at her church.

As much as Kelly's family loved their urban Seattle community, where they knew all their neighbors, they missed their Idaho home. When her children were in fourth and seventh grade, they moved back to New Plymouth, Idaho, where Kelly once again became involved in her children's school.

The school superintendent asked her to start a volunteer program to make parents feel welcome. At that time, the Idaho Department of Education had started an AmeriCorps VISTA program. Kelly was selected to be a VISTA coordinator for a local America Reads program, which she did for over two years. Then she moved into a regional VISTA leadership position from 1997 to 2000, while her kids were in high school. She attended a handful of college classes, but was never a full-time student.

After AmeriCorps VISTA, she worked with the Malheur County Commission on Children and Families. Three years later she became the director of the Commission. The Commission proved to be a perfect organizational model for Kelly to utilize her community building and organizational skills. In the past, the role of the Commission had been simply to give out competitive grants to support existing children's programs. Even before becoming director, Kelly was changing this model, from acting simply as a funding agent to connecting and empowering people and developing programs.

In the early 2000s, the communities around Ontario, Oregon were struggling with issues of child abuse and neglect. Much of this was the result of the 1991 opening of the Snake River Correctional Institution (SRCI), which soon became Oregon's largest prison, housing over 2,000 medium security inmates just five miles from Ontario.

With the community facing major issues that were not being addressed by existing programs, Kelly and her coworker, Angie Uptmor, began encouraging the development of new programs to support the troubled families of current and former inmates. The first was the Children of Incarcerated Parents Initiative.

In 2006, the Commission worked with the Sheriff's Office and leaders of the SRCI to promote the idea of a Children's Relief Nursery. People said, "You can't do a relief nursery here. You're too rural." Despite the resistance, Kelly and Angie were able to lay the groundwork for the creation of the relief nursery. The biggest challenge they faced was hiring the right person to serve as director. They lured Kathie Collins, whom they knew to be a strong leader, out of a communications business. Kathie and the Treasure Valley Children's Relief Nursery have been very successful since their 2009 opening in meeting the needs of at risk families in Malheur County.

"I am a team player," says Kelly. "One of the challenges I have is that people think I am supporting projects that were my ideas. That's rarely the case. I'm good at listening and supporting other people's good ideas."

Another challenge facing Ontario was the arrival of gangs. Kids were being recruited by gangs when they were in middle school. Kelly and Angie traveled to Bend, Eugene, and Medford to visit after-school programs which had been formed to provide positive youth activities in those communities.

With the support of the Commission, the Boys and Girls Club of Western Treasure Valley was founded in 2008. The organization now serves over 1,500 school-aged kids and is playing a major role in those communities in reversing a very troubling school dropout rate of over 50%. Kelly is thrilled to have Club Director Matt Sorensen leading the organization and is inspired by its success. "It's about the common good and vulnerable kids. If you raise people to be healthy adults, you improve the economy."

Where there is poverty, there is often hunger. When Kelly started on the Commission, there was one food bank and one distribution site in the community. Kelly was part of a team that hosted community forums in 2004, which revealed the need for more food bank locations. With the help of Oregon Food Bank, there is now a local warehouse as well as distribution pantries throughout the two-county area.

Back in 2005, Kelly read an article about the Ford Family Foundation's Leadership Institute Program. She participated in the program in 2006-07 and since then has served on the Community Ambassador Team (CAT). As a CAT member, she has helped facilitate new leadership cohorts.

Later, she served as a Ford Community Fellow from 2011 to 2014 and led community building efforts. According to Kelly, the Leadership Institute has developed a proven framework to train over 5,000 people in rural and economically challenged Oregon communities.

In 2013, statewide funding for the Commission on Children and Families ended, and the program was replaced by Early Learning Hubs. Kelly helped design the new system to address the needs for education, health and related services for low-income and at-risk children and their families. Malheur, Baker and Wallowa Counties joined to form the Eastern Oregon Community Based Services Hub, housed in the offices of the Malheur Education Service District (ESD).

Steve Phillips had been hired to replace the retiring ESD Superintendent in 2012. When the time came to name a leader for this newly created service hub, Phillips approached Kelly Poe. "I don't understand the things you do," he told Kelly. "But keep doing them!"

Kelly became the director of the new organization. She reflects on her new job. "We are trying to serve three large counties. There's not enough money, but it's not about the money. It's about finding proven strategies that will work in rural eastern Oregon."

Kelly's current priorities focus on those things outside the K-12 education system that impact kids and families. She is committed to a "cradle to career" partnership between schools and the community, focusing on healthy births, kindergarten readiness, school attendance, and high school graduation. Her primary focus is on outreach to families not connected to positive community supports such as Head Start programs, neighborhoods, libraries and churches. According to Kelly, "Not everyone needs services, but everyone needs to be connected."

Looking back at her success with the Commission, Kelly reflects:

> *The agency achieved its greatest success when its focus moved from funding to mobilizing communities and leveraging resources. It's about relationships, not money. The more you can focus on the common good—versus your organization's mission statement—the more you will achieve your mission.*

As I walk out of the coffee shop in downtown Ontario, I am anything but bored. Kelly Poe may never have directed a private nonprofit organization; nonetheless, her compassion, listening skills, and ability to inspire others to tackle tough problems are making an impact. The problems have not completely disappeared, but there are innovative new programs, led by good people, which are addressing those problems and making a huge difference in this small Oregon community.

IV

Giving Back

"From everyone who has been given much, much more will be demanded."

Luke 12:48

The passion to give back is a powerful force for many nonprofit leaders, inextricably linked with who they are. This passion manifests itself differently in different people.

The Doctor
Dr. Jill Ginsberg had everything—a loving family and a successful medical career. But her life took a dramatic turn when she answered a pastor's call to start a community health center for people who could not afford health care. And her giving did not stop there...

The Counselor
As one of nine children of a Baptist preacher and a demanding mother, **Margaret Carter** was driven by John Kennedy's challenge to give back to her country. From Fuller Brush Company salesperson and church pianist at age 12 to community advocate at age 77, Margaret Carter has never stopped giving back.

The Coach
Bob Lieberman was taught by his Jewish parents in Chicago to live in a way that does not support injustice. In his youth he fought injustice marching with Martin Luther King. In Grants Pass, Oregon, he transferred his passion for justice to changing the lives of troubled adolescents.

The Foster Parent
Mary Collard felt very special and secure as a child growing up in South Carolina. She knew from an early age she wanted to have children and also adopt. When she was uprooted to a strange and different world in Baker City, Oregon, she found a new home, bringing warmth and security not only to her own children, but to hundreds more.

The Doctor

> "She needed a doctor. A doctor walked in the door. It fulfilled destiny."
>
> Dr. Jill Ginsberg
> January 2012

Growing up in New Jersey, Jill Ginsberg's father was a strong influence in her life. He had gone to law school, but before he started to practice law, he heeded a call to help with the family gas station in Hoboken, New Jersey. Many years later he became a Legal Aid attorney.

He had a profound influence on Jill's ideas of justice, power and fairness. "He was a grease-under-the-fingernails guy who was devoted to the idea that the underdog is king. He taught me that people who cannot defend themselves deserve a champion."

Jill pursued Latin American studies at Barnard College. Her worldview was further solidified when she spent six months in South America and was inspired by the doctor and champion of the underdog, Che Guevara.

She got her M.D. and public health degree at UCSF. After doing tribal work on a reservation in Neah Bay, Washington, she moved to Portland in 1995 and joined Kaiser Permanente, focusing on women's healthcare and on groups with special needs like diabetes.

10 years ago, Dr. Jill Ginsberg's life would have been considered a great example of the personal and professional rewards of hard work and dedication. She had achieved her goal of becoming a doctor and was focusing her practice in areas that matched her beliefs. "I was just fine with what I was doing, taking care of patients at KP and spending time with my family."

When Hurricane Katrina hit New Orleans, Jill was appalled by the apathetic response of our government and citizens. As a healthcare professional, she wanted to do something. She had heard about the work of a woman in Northeast Portland named Pastor Mary, who had sold her vacation home to support Katrina victims moving to Portland from New Orleans. She did this by paying for their transportation to Portland and then providing them lodging and meeting their basic needs for three months while they were getting back on their feet.

Inspired by Pastor Mary's work, Jill arranged to meet her. When they met, Pastor Mary told Jill, "We need a free clinic."

Jill's first reaction was negative. "It was never an aspiration of mine to start a free clinic. I saw it as a band-aid approach."

But Pastor Mary had other ideas. She walked Jill up the street to the house that was to become the free clinic and asked, "When are you going to start?"

Jill was not looking for a life-changing project, but Pastor Mary was very persuasive. Jill smiles when she tells the story. "She needed a doctor. A doctor walked in. It fulfilled destiny."

It was November 2005 when Pastor Mary walked Jill up to the house. The North by Northeast Community Health Center opened in August 2006 in that same house. The concept of the North by Northeast Community Health Center was very different from a typical free clinic. The focus was on chronic issues like diabetes and high blood pressure.

"That is what we heard from the community that was needed, as opposed to an urgent care clinic. We wanted to be more than a clinic. We wanted to be a center for community health."

Jill asked many people to help, and the center received some good publicity early on. For two years, Jill volunteered full time for the center, while continuing to work 26 hours per week for Kaiser. In 2007 she received a seven-month sabbatical from Kaiser and hired the first staff member for the clinic, Roslyn Farrington. Currently there are five paid staff members. The doctors and nurses are all volunteers.

The budget went from 0 to $50,000 in 2006 and to over $300,000 in 2013. By 2013 the clinic was seeing 130 patients per month, 80% of whom had chronic health conditions such as hypertension, heart disease, asthma and diabetes.

Many community leaders, along with all the major health systems, stepped up to join the effort and ensure its success. The center has a dedicated board of directors, led by people who have standing in the community. It was the board that was determined to listen to the community and deliver services that the community wanted. They did focus groups, and the results of those focus groups and community conversations set the course for the center's work.

Their fundraising efforts started modestly, with a column in the Oregonian asking for help. From that column came thousands of dollars, volunteers and requests to submit grant proposals. All the local health providers stepped up with financial support, volunteers, lab services and technical assistance. In 2013 the North by Northeast Center was supported by two dozen volunteer doctors, a dedicated group of nurses and over 80 volunteers in total.

Through the efforts of the staff and the volunteers, thousands of people with high blood pressure and diabetes have been able to keep their conditions under control. Serious and even deadly complications have been prevented, along with visits to the local emergency room.

But Jill Ginsberg's story doesn't end there. Just as her father inspired Jill to be a champion of the underdog, her mother unknowingly inspired her to extend a hand of generosity to strangers.

Jill's mother was a young girl living in Berlin when Hitler came to power. Her affluent Jewish family lost everything. She was able to escape with her life, but lived in Britain with strangers for years before moving to America. It was a traumatic time for her, living as an enemy alien with constant uncertainty of what the next day would bring. She carried that sense of deprivation with her for the rest of her life.

In spite of her father's salary as an attorney working for Legal Aid, Jill's mother's past experiences made it hard for her to feel financially secure. Until she was older, Jill thought her family was poor. Her father died suddenly while Jill was in high school, and Jill had to work her way through college, with no help from her mother.

When her mother passed away and left her a sum of money, Jill decided to use some of the money to do something that her mother could never have imagined—to purge herself of that sense of poverty and deprivation by walking up to strangers and giving them $100 bills. She did this every day during the month of October, 2010. She continued to give away $100 bills at least once a week through 2011 and 2012, totaling approximately $15,000 in gifts. "It became part of my life, in a way similar to a spiritual practice, and required a lot of observation, processing and self-reflection."

Jill describes the experience as helping her escape from a prison of perceived poverty that had shut her mother off from the rest of the world. During this time, Jill kept a blog, "Hundreds of Hundreds," describing her experiences. Her story also inspired others to give, some of whom shared their stories on the website.

As Dr. Jill Ginsberg reflects on the unlikely events of the last eight years of her life, she shares a few lessons she has learned from over 30 years in medicine, which were reinforced while giving away $100 bills:

> *You can never know what is going on with a person from a glance. People who look just like you and me can be on the brink of disaster and despair.*

People have a fundamental need to be recognized. Often the money is like a secret handshake, a way of saying, "I see you. What you are going through matters to me." We can never go wrong by showing genuine caring to a stranger.

In life, gifts often come from unexpected sources. Jill's mother gave her the gift that ironically helped Jill break her mother's mold and discover the joy of giving to strangers—both from her wallet and from her heart.

The Counselor

> "It's not all the glamour and glitz that make you successful. It's the ability to clean bathrooms one minute and sit in the boardroom the next."
>
> Margaret Carter
> August 2012

Margaret Carter grew up in Shreveport, Louisiana in a family of nine children. She attributes her core values to her father, a Baptist minister, and a mother who instilled in her the value of service at an early age. Margaret reflects:

> *With grace and confidence, my father advised his children to follow John Kennedy's challenge: "Ask not what your country can do for you; ask what you can do for your country." Put in more pragmatic, everyday language, "You cannot live here without giving back!"*

At the age of five, Margaret kicked off a long career in politics by distributing voter registration cards. At age 12 her mother said, "You are a great salesperson. You need to get a job." So she began selling Fuller brushes. Also at age 12, Margaret's mother informed her, "You will take music lessons." Within three years

Margaret was playing piano for her church. Piano helped her learn to express herself with passion in front of an audience; then, in her high school debate class, Margaret learned to sell ideas.

The values that were instilled in Margaret and the talents she developed in the early years of her life set the tone for the rest of her life. She reflects, "It became my passion at an early age to work for my country."

Margaret was able to channel that passion into a job at Southeast Portland Community Center. She had to raise money in order to fund the programs that the community needed. "I learned early on that you need to understand the budget in order to answer the call to any area of poverty. You follow the money. You fund the policies."

Her father never finished high school, and her mother never got past ninth grade, but six of their nine children went to college, four received their BAs and Margaret earned her master's. Margaret was class salutatorian at her high school and attended Grambling State College for over two years before her education was interrupted by marriage and children.

Unfortunately, her marriage of 13 years ended in domestic violence, when she fled their home at 3 o'clock in the morning with five babies in tow and only a hundred dollars in her pocket. In December 1967, she relocated to Portland with no money, those five babies, and friends who were generous enough to take them in. She immediately landed a job at the local 88 cent store. Later, she was hired as a teacher's assistant for Portland Public Schools. Bill White, the principal at Highland (now

King) Elementary, had heard compliments about Margaret's ability to teach reading through phonetics. He believed in her and encouraged her to become a teacher. She protested—"But I have five babies to support!"

Mr. White replied by giving Margaret the business card of a friend from the Oregon Department of Vocational Rehabilitation. Margaret became very angry at the thought of being referred to a welfare program. No one in her family had ever been on welfare, and she was not about to be the first. Mr. White responded, "This is not welfare."

After stewing about it for over a week, Margaret followed his advice and went to see his friend, Mary Wendy Roberts. After a long conversation, Mary Wendy recommended seeing a psychologist friend of hers. That really set Margaret off. "First I'm referred to a welfare program and now a psychologist. I left that meeting in a huff!"

Fortunately, she agreed to meet with the psychologist. Her first words to the psychologist were, "I'm not crazy!"

The psychologist convinced her to utilize the Vocational Rehabilitation program that was available for just such situations and circumstances. Two years later she finished her BA at Portland State University. After graduating, she taught reading at Albina Youth Opportunity School.

Driven as she has been her whole life, a bachelor's degree was not enough. Margaret was determined to help the high-risk families in her community understand the dynamics of the social structures and how to access them successfully. She knew that in order to do that she needed a higher skill level in psychology and sociology.

With perseverance and determination, she sought out university settings that would help her meet this goal. She discovered a professor who was offering a program in counseling in the Portland area. Dr. Edward F. Fuller from Oregon State University, in partnership with the Northwest Regional Educational Laboratory, created a cohort; Margaret went back to get her master's degree. She achieved her MA in counseling in 1973.

In the spring of 1973, she began a long and fruitful relationship with Portland Community College, where she worked as a counselor from 1973 to 1999. During that 26-year period, she was very active in politics as a state legislator, where she served as co-chair of the Ways and Means Committee. A reporter once told her that he knew she could sing, but didn't know she could do budgets. "Little did he know that I was selling Fuller brushes before I ever learned to play the piano and balancing a budget before he was born!"

During this time, Margaret remarried and inherited her second husband's four kids, resulting in a total of nine children. "It was as if I had three sets of twins overnight." But that never stopped her—it didn't even slow her down. Margaret understood mothering and working.

In 1999 the Urban League of Portland was having significant problems. They asked Margaret to head up the League, but she was initially unsure and not totally convinced that she could do it. A philanthropist approached her and said, "If you take the job with the Urban League, I will commit $10,000 from my foundation for the support of the League."

Margaret took the job and worked tirelessly to raise money to bring the Urban League back to its feet. "In the morning I would clean the bathrooms and go to work. In the afternoon I would go home, take a shower and head back to the boardroom to raise money."

When I interview Margaret in August 2012, she is serving as Director of Community Engagement for Oregon's Department of Human Services. It is ironic that she was introduced to the agency as a client of their Voc-Rehab program and then ended up as their community engagement director!

As I leave the interview, her final words are, "Today, I'm 77 years old and still going strong! I've never been away from work for any significant amount of time. I'm afraid to retire, if retirement means I can't continue to make a difference."

Many people feel at age 65 (or earlier) that they have earned the right to move on from work to the next phase in their life: retirement. After 65 years of work, from selling Fuller brushes to developing budgets for the State of Oregon, Margaret Carter still isn't ready to quit. The result is a win for the state of Oregon. Somewhere, Margaret's mother is smiling!

Giving Back

The Coach

"I am not a believer in doing it alone. Even though I love the passion and idealism of Don Quixote chasing windmills, to me it's more about trying to find where we can come together to make a difference."

Bob Lieberman
September 2014

As I enter Bob Lieberman's office at Kairos in Grants Pass, Oregon, I immediately notice two plaques on the wall. The first is a plaque congratulating Bob for his 35 years of service, awarded in 2012. The second plaque refers to plans A, B, and C.

As Bob walks in, I ask about the second plaque and how it relates to his line of work—serving youth with severe mental and emotional problems. He explains to me that the three plans are the core of Collaborative Problem Solving, a different approach to dealing with troubled youths. Plan A is to bypass the youth and solve the problem "the adult way." This is the traditional disciplinarian approach, where the adult makes the rules and punishments while the wishes and emotions of the youth are ignored. Plan B is more empathetic and involves collaborative problem solving with the young adults by taking their perspective into account. Plan C amounts to dropping expectations and ignoring the problem. At first glance plan B may not seem as direct and efficient as plan A, or as easy (in the short term) as plan C, but Bob believes it is more efficient and sustainable in the long run.

I learn a lot about Bob Lieberman simply listening to him talk about Plan B. Bob is a man who has gathered values and bits of wisdom throughout his life and passes them along to his growing organization, with each new hire and with all staff and youth participants. He holds these values close to his heart, and they have served him well.

I would love to spend the afternoon talking leadership with Bob. His understanding seems very rooted and his convictions deep. But I am even more curious to understand where the man came from and who he is.

Bob is a second-generation American Jew whose grandparents fled the Cossacks in eastern Europe. He grew up in Chicago and was raised by his parents in the folk school tradition. They bickered a lot but raised their children well. His mother was an activist and early feminist. On his deathbed, his father said he had a falling out with God in the 1940s.

> *The whisper in the family was that both my parents were "pinkos." My bar mitzvah consisted of two big parties. But I was taught that because the Jewish people were horrendously persecuted throughout history, it is our place to live in a way that does not support injustice.*

When he was 10 years old, Bob marched with Martin Luther

King in Chicago. He protested Vietnam and was tear-gassed while involved in civil rights activities. He supported the Great Society and was a volunteer driver for Eugene McCarthy in 1968.

Bob went to high school in Chicago and graduated early, two months before his 17th birthday. He was a student at the University of Illinois in 1970 during the campus uprisings. Today, he laments that fewer than two in ten new employees at Kairos have even heard of Kent State or the 1968 Chicago convention.

Despite the distractions of the student movement, Bob made every effort to focus on his English major. He recalls a course in 17th century English literature, where he had done all the reading and scored well on the midterm. When taking a final exam, which was composed of questions probing minute factual details of the reading and lectures, Bob answered in a way that showed his understanding of the subject matter. He failed the exam. When he explained the circumstances and made a case for a barely passing grade, his professor responded, "I've had a point system for 30 years. You failed."

Bob's response was swift and dramatic. "I dropped out of school in 1970. It was the best decision I ever made."

Bob became interested in helping other children at a very early age. When he was six or seven years old, he would watch parents and their kids interact in the grocery store. Even then, he knew when certain parents were doing the wrong thing. Armed with interest and good instincts for working with kids, he earned money as a babysitter at age twelve.

After dropping out of college in 1970, Bob visited friends from Portland who lived in a house above Skyline Drive. He was hooked and soon moved to Portland. He got a daycare job in Forest Grove and in 1974 worked in residential treatment at the Christie School.

After several years of working hard for low pay, he finally acknowledged that he needed a degree in order to make a decent salary. He was accepted at Lewis and Clark College, where he graduated in secondary education. A highlight was retaking the 17th century English literature class and loving it!

After graduating, Bob applied for jobs in several rural school districts. "I knew very clearly that I wanted to work with middle school students, but no one would hire me because of my long hair."

Discouraged with his inability to land a teaching position, Bob applied for a residential treatment position in Grants Pass, where he was hired in 1977 by the Southern Oregon Adolescent Study and Treatment Center.

He never left the organization, which changed its name several years ago to Kairos. Bob explains the name change and the very careful thought that went into it. Kairos comes from the Greek word meaning the moment in time when change is most possible. According to Bob:

> *The opportunity to make a difference in every moment if we know what we are thinking and know the child... the moment when opportunity and action intersect...has guided my approach to working with young people for years.*

The new name was perfect.

Bob becomes animated as he tells stories about the young people he has served:

> *There was a family in town where I saw a transformation in one hour. The parents were going to send their 17-year-old out of state to a residential boarding school because they thought they had tried everything. At a critical point in the relationship, I was able to coach the father about Collaborative Problem Solving. The turnaround in the relationship happened almost instantaneously.*

At the time of our interview, Bob is in the midst of a capital campaign to fund two building projects, focused on Kairos' community-based services model. In addition to several major foundation grants, Bob has teamed with Dr. Dick Phillips, a retired OHSU psychiatrist. Dr. Phillips had earlier committed to using his connections to seek private funding for an acute care unit for children at the local hospital. An advisory committee recommended against the approach, indicating that community-based care was a greater need, but the hospital went ahead with plans for the acute care facility. Dr. Phillips secured two major gifts, but the hospital never followed through, and the gifts were returned.

Eight years later, Bob contacted Dr. Phillips and told him about Kairos' plans to build a new residential facility linked with community-based services for young people and families. Dr. Phillips agreed that the linked model was the way to go and offered to help Bob raise private funds. Their partnership began with a luncheon that Dr. Phillips hosted at the Arlington Club in Portland, where Bob spoke about the need for community-based mental health services for kids in Southern Oregon. With several commitments in hand and with the help of Dr. Phillips, Bob plans to kick off the fundraising campaign in the fall of 2014.

Bob Lieberman's commitment to community-based mental health treatment for children runs deep. Equally deep is his commitment to Southern Oregon. Over the past 10 years he has been recruited several times to move to urban areas to lead programs, including a salary that would more than double what he makes at Kairos; but has consistently rejected the offers and remained in Southern Oregon.

His experience in Southern Oregon has not been without its frustrations, however. Reflecting on his work with other Southern Oregon nonprofits, he acknowledges:

> *The idea of not competing for grants and funding ended about 10 years ago. Over time the issue of turf has become stronger. We talk about collaboration, but I'm not sure we've done it in reality. On the other hand, I'm happy not to be doing this in the Portland metropolitan area, where competition in the nonprofit world is fierce. It's draining to be up there in meetings.*

Bob realizes that not all change can occur at the local level:

> *I want to make a difference. That has always motivated me. In October 2005 I worked very hard to push for the Children's System Change Initiative, which eventually became House Bill 2144 in Oregon. It passed despite some*

strong opposition.

As we end the interview, Bob reflects upon people like Dick Phillips, whom he has learned a lot from and worked with in partnership to achieve success:

> *In the end, I am not a believer in doing it alone. Even though I love the passion and the idealism of Don Quixote chasing windmills, for me it's more about trying to find where we can come together to make a difference.*

Bob doesn't say it, but I think to myself, "That sounds a lot like plan B!"

Author's note: After a successful capital campaign and a carefully planned transition, Bob left Kairos in 2017 to start a consulting firm, Lieberman Group, Inc. He continues to train and publish and has remained active in community collaborations in southern Oregon, statewide and nationally.

The Foster Parent

"My husband jokes that I am the only person he knows who answers the phone when there is a wrong number and gets into a conversation with the other person to offer help."

Mary Collard
November 2015

Mary Collard was born and raised in West Columbia, South Carolina, the youngest of three children. Her parents were both high school music teachers. Her father was a band director who wrote school songs for several schools and later went on to become principal and superintendent.

Mary's father died when Mary was fifteen. He had always "taken care of things" for the family, so his best friend, who was their banker, helped her mother sort things out.

Mary reflects on her childhood:

> *I felt so special and secure. I never knew of anything different. I always wanted to be a wife and a mom...to have both birth children and adopted children. It saddened me that there were children who did not have that love and security.*

Mary was always active in music, dance and gymnastics and ultimately became a competitive gymnast in the Junior Olympic program. Her gymnastics career ended with an ankle injury. In spite of the injury, she continued teaching and coaching gymnastics in college PE classes while attending college in South Carolina.

One of her gymnastic students was a big, burly guy who coached football. In spite of their physical mismatch (she weighed under 100 pounds), she fell in love with Bryan. After a few years in South Carolina, Bryan decided to return to his home state of Oregon. Mary says she had no choice. "I was madly in love with the guy and decided to pick up and leave. I was the first in the family to fly the nest. It broke my mother's heart."

The first winter was a rough one. When they were driving from Boise to Baker City, the rugged, treeless landscape felt like another planet to Mary. She recalls thinking, "What have I done? Where is this place?"

It didn't get any better when they arrived in town. "Main Street in Baker City was the most foreign thing I had ever seen. The biggest impact was how flippin' cold it was. It didn't stop snowing!"

Mary's first job in Oregon was interpreting for a deaf child in a Baker City School. To this day, she loves to stay in contact with the children she assisted.

At the end of the school year, Mary received a phone call that her paternal grandfather had passed away. She was still living with Bryan's parents, as they were not yet married. "I looked at the principal and at Bryan and said, 'I'm out of here. I need to go back to South Carolina, and I ain't coming back.'"

Later that summer, Bryan drove his motorcycle across the country. In September they got married and settled in Columbia, South Carolina, where Bryan became a police officer. A year later, in 1986, they had a son, followed by another son and a daughter. Mary was a stay-at-home mom and taught gymnastics in the evening with all of her little ones in tow.

Mary remembers Bryan leaving home on Sundays for work wearing a bulletproof vest in 100-plus degree weather for the midnight shift. She was so relieved when he would return home the next day. He loved his work, but it was very dangerous and challenging at times. In the summer of 1993, they traveled to Baker City for Bryan's 10-year high school reunion. The town looked very different to Mary this time. "I was settled, with three kids. This little town didn't look so bad after all. It seemed like a great place to raise children, so we moved a month later."

It still took some time for Mary to adjust to her new home. "I got here and still felt like an outsider. I cried every day for the first two years. I couldn't fit in and feel that it was my place. I was just the wife of a guy who grew up here."

Once the kids started school, things got better. Mary got involved in church and in school. She also babysat for a friend who had adopted foster kids. "I told her she was crazy," reflects Mary. Six months later Mary and Bryan were certified to provide foster care and got the first two of many foster children to come into the Collard family.

Having foster kids opened up Mary's eyes to a new world—the court system and the legal system. She wanted to have a relationship with the birth family and ended up mentoring the birth mothers whenever possible. The children Mary and Bryan fostered had CASA (Court Appointed Special Advocates) volunteer advocates. According to Mary, "I experienced CASA first hand. CASA made a huge difference, and I became interested in the behind-the-scenes processes."

The US Supreme Court mandated CASA for every county in the nation in 1993. CASA was set up to support neglected/at risk children by pairing each child with a volunteer advocate. There was no funding attached to the mandate, however. CASA was established in Baker City in 1996.

In 2001, Mary was approached by the CASA board to serve as program director. She reflects:

> *It was like the sky had opened up. I told the interview committee that I had no experience or interest in grant writing, but I could definitely learn. In spite of that, I was hired and became director in 2001.*

Mary's first successful grant, from the Leo Adler Foundation, came shortly after she was hired. She describes it as a validating experience. After that, grant writing became a fun challenge involving "facts, figures, and storytelling."

Today, CASA of Eastern Oregon serves three counties. About 10% of its funding comes from the state, with the remainder evenly split between grants and the local community. According to Mary, Baker County has a strong partnership spirit, and the community fundraisers are lucrative. Malheur County is more challenging, as it is spread out, sits right on the Idaho border, and has many other competing nonprofits. Union County is the newest addition to CASA of Eastern Oregon.

In 2015, CASA of Eastern Oregon served over 250 children, with 2.5 equivalent staff and 55 volunteers. Describing the challenge of serving three large counties in eastern Oregon with such a small staff, Mary laughs, "I've always been able to figure out a way to pull something together. It's not a bang-down-the-door process to get the attention we need. I'm always up for a good party and enjoy speaking to the public anywhere I can."

Although Mary is proud of the numbers, it is the stories of children who have been touched by the program that truly inspire her. She tells a story of three brothers with significant problems—severe abuse and abuse of each other. The original volunteer advocated for separate placements, which was not a popular stand to take; but she knew these children and what they needed. As a result, each child had a different CASA advocate and separate foster home.

One of the children was adopted by a family in a neighboring state. The three CASA volunteers continued to work together and advocate for the boys. Then the youngest child was adopted. The family kept in touch with the other kids and later adopted the second child. All three children now have homes, with two living together and in contact with the third.

Mary heard that one of the boys needed a bike to ride in the country.

> *I sent out an email to our CASA friends. In twenty minutes we got a donation to purchase a great mountain bike and all of the safety gear. To this day, 10 years later, I have a picture of the boy on his bike, with a handwritten thank-you note hanging in my office.*

This kind of generosity happens in all three counties. In addition to volunteers, there is a network of people who will step forward to support a child. Recently, Mary became aware of a non-CASA child who couldn't go to recess because he didn't have a warm coat. She sent out an email to Rotary Club members, and the child got a coat for recess that same day.

According to Mary:

> *Our mission at CASA is to speak for a child's best interest in court, but for me it is every child in any situation. My husband jokes that I am the only person he knows who answers the phone when there is a wrong number and gets into a conversation with the other person to offer help.*

Mary's advice to people who work with at-risk children is to "always picture children in the center of the room and remember why we are here. We all have different roads but the same end—a safe, loving and stable home for kids."

As we end the interview, Mary reflects:

> *I always go back to my roots, to that warm feeling I had when I was a little girl. When I am working hard and*

looking for money to fund our program, I remember that warm feeling. Everyone should have memories of that feeling from somewhere in their life. It is why I do this work.

V

Advocacy

In 1976, Webster's dictionary defined advocacy as "the act of pleading or defending a cause." Today, the first definition that appears after an internet search adds the word "publicly." The five nonprofit leaders featured in this chapter all excel in their passion for supporting a cause. Some do so very publicly; others, like many in the nonprofit world, do their work away from the public spotlight.

The Vista Volunteer
When a recession hit Oregon in the early 1980s, **Rachel Bristol** had only four dollars in her pocket. She volunteered at a fledgling food distribution program. 29 years later she retired, after leading efforts to distribute over a billion pounds of food in Oregon.

The Justice Seeker
Through his support for Latinos in Oregon and around the country, **Ramon Ramirez** has witnessed both victories and heartbreaking defeats in the struggle for acceptance and economic justice.

The Believer
After reluctantly agreeing to "temporarily" lead an agency serving addicts, **Rita Sullivan** ended up spending 35 years convincing patients and the public that addiction is curable, and that families of addicts should remain together.

The Quiet Leader
Brenda Johnson speaks softly, but her life experiences have instilled in her a passion for justice when it comes to helping people who don't have access to primary medical, dental and mental health services.

The Writer
With years of experience doing community work overseas and in the nation's capital, **Rich Wandschneider** settled in the mountains of Eastern Oregon and began a new career: bringing the arts to his newfound home.

Advocacy

The Vista Volunteer

"We need to get the profits back in the hands of the people who are making the widgets. I don't know if we can change the game, but we can keep trying."

Rachel Bristol
June 2012

When I interview Rachel Bristol in June 2012, she is in her last week as CEO for the Oregon Food Bank. She has served a long time as a crusader against hunger in Oregon, first as a 27-year-old volunteer who picked up and distributed food donations to various food banks, and later as CEO for a statewide organization that helps one in five households in Oregon and southwest Washington.

The Food Bank distributes food from a variety of sources through four branch locations (Beaverton, Ontario, Tillamook and Portland), 16 independent local food banks, and 923 partner organizations. As a result of two successful campaigns, the Food Bank has grown under Bristol's leadership from a 10,000 square-foot facility to four facilities encompassing more than 155,000 square feet.

Arnie Gardner, Nike executive and chair of the Food Bank at the time of Bristol's announced retirement, credits her with overseeing the distribution of over one billion pounds of food during her 29 year career. "She enlisted everyone from the governor to everyday citizens in the campaign, not only to deliver food where it was needed, but also to advocate for policies that attack hunger's root causes."

Her work has not gone unnoticed. She has received many local and national awards for her work, including an honorary doctorate in public service from the University of Portland. In 2010, she received the Paul G. Allen Foundation's Founders Award. In 2009 she received the Dick Goebel Public Service Award from Feeding America. That year she was also named "Most Admired Nonprofit CEO" by the Portland Business Journal and was awarded the Distinguished Alumnus Award from the University of Oregon. The Oregonian Editorial Board, on May 1, 2012, said it best: "The Oregon Food Bank is a point of Oregon pride, a marker of our sense of obligation toward each other."

The Oregon Food Bank's powerhouse leader has been plagued in recent years by arthritis and chronic fatigue syndrome. When I ask about her coming retirement, she responds, "This will be the first time I've had the summer off since I was a kid."

Having learned about Rachel Bristol's illustrious career prior to the interview, I am eager to learn more about her childhood. Fortunately, Rachel is more than willing to reminisce about her unlikely rise to prominence.

Her father grew up in Appalachia, catching raccoons and

squirrels to eat. When he was just 12 years old, his father died, leaving him and his six sisters behind. He quit school and lied about his age so he could work in a linen mill. Later he moved to Washington, where he worked in a paper mill. Rachel's mother grew up in a family of North Florida sharecroppers. Her maternal grandmother, the wife of a minister and dairy farmer, worked in a Coca-Cola factory.

Rachel's parents married the day her father got out of high school, when he was 18; her mother was 16. Her father could fix anything. He knew everything about paper and bags. Rachel had three older brothers. Her parents often said, "We were poor but never hungry."

Her family lived off the land. Rachel learned to can peas, beans and tuna from her grandparents. "My granddaddy really knew the true meaning of Christianity: give whatever you have."

Her parents read every page of the newspaper and talked about it with the kids. Her father had some favorite sayings: "Do whatever needs to be done. Take as long as it takes. And do it right!"

You could see the light coming through the walls in their first house in Beaverton. When Rachel was 13 or 14, her parents moved the family from Beaverton to Newberg.

"It was a fluke that I got into college," reflects Rachel. "I was a volleyball player, and my PE teacher applied for a scholarship for me at OSU."

Academic success did not come quickly to Rachel. She quit

college and went to live with her boyfriend, working at the Forest Service through the Comprehensive Employment and Training Act (CETA) and the Youth Conservation Corps. Later she enrolled at Linn Benton Community College (LBCC) in a program for women in nontraditional roles. This time she followed through and became certified as a forklift operator.

Throughout her youth, Rachel got involved in many causes: leading a membership drive to purchase a food co-op in Corvallis, starting a recycling program at LBCC's campus, working to get the Equal Rights Amendment passed at OSU, and participating in anti-nuclear demonstrations. She speaks of her lifelong passion to represent the "have-nots." "We need to get the profits back in the hands of the people who are making the widgets. I don't know if we can change the game, but we can keep trying."

Rachel laughs when she reflects, "My future board chair at Oregon Food Bank was PGE's leader at Trojan when I was dragged out of the facility when performing an act of civil disobedience!"

At the age of 25 she went back to school, attending the University of Oregon and studying organizational and community development through the Community Service and Public Affairs program. As a student she got involved in US Bank's "Let's Bag Hunger" campaign. Her father's company donated half a million bags!

She graduated from the University of Oregon in 1982. That was a turning point in her life. "I had a choice—live on a commune or move to the city and try to change things."

Advocacy

She chose the latter, showing up at her brother's door in Portland with just four dollars in her pocket at the height of one of Oregon's worst economic downturns. It was a difficult time; she was on unemployment and food stamps for five months. At that time, her parents and grandparents took her in and brought in all her friends with her, treating them like family.

Later that year she joined Volunteers in Service to America (VISTA) and was assigned to the fledgling Oregon Food Share Project. She worked with 13 other VISTAs, begging for food and transportation and developing a regional interagency food bank program. With many Oregonians unemployed and struggling financially, the food bank would find food otherwise bound for the landfill and direct it to agencies to feed the hungry.

At that time, President Reagan had approved the release of federal surplus cheese. Rachel called on gleaners for labor and worked with volunteer truckers to figure out the challenge of food distribution. The State of Oregon took notice of the work Rachel was doing and asked her to develop a plan for commodity food distribution. She responded by creating what would become a national model for food banking.

In 1984 they had their first warehouse. Rachel was right at home. "I was the forklift operator!"

Also at that time, Senator Mark Hatfield helped save the Emergency Food Assistance Program. In the mid-1980s they were serving 200,000 food boxes a year. Over time, the interagency food bank she developed as a VISTA volunteer grew larger and more successful. Today, the number of food boxes served annually is well over a million.

In 1987 the interagency food bank merged with another food bank, and Rachel was named the acting director of the merger, which was named the Oregon Food Bank. After the board hired an outside person to be executive director and it didn't work out, Rachel became the permanent executive director. One of her first acts as executive director was to lead the organization in redefining its mission—from distributing food to eliminating hunger.

Her new executive role did not douse the fire that drove Rachel to follow her calling. Her voice rises, "It disturbs me how huge the hunger problem is now—much worse than in the economic hard times of the '80s. To combat it we need to harness the power of community engagement."

Looking back on her long career as she anticipates retirement, Rachel reflects:

> *I have been honored to 'grow up' with the Oregon Food Bank and its network. We've faced a growing number of people in need and changing resources, but we've never lost sight of our mission—to end hunger in both the short and long term.*

Rachel Bristol's impact on hunger in Oregon has been huge. "If you want to change the world, you have to convince a lot of people that it needs changing."

In 29 years, Rachel has convinced a lot of people. She has gone from an idealistic volunteer with four dollars in her pocket to a CEO working out of a 100,000 square-foot corporate office, serving a board of corporate and community leaders who have brought business credibility and millions of dollars in resources to the Oregon Food Bank.

But success has not spoiled Rachel. As I prepare to leave, she reflects, "There's a part of me that's still the wide-eyed kid that asks myself, 'Did I really lead us through all those years?'"

You did, Rachel. Yes, you surely did.

The Justice Seeker

"I am convinced that there is a better world out there—a world of respect, dignity and diversity."

Ramon Ramirez
March 2012

I am a little nervous as I drive down to Woodburn to meet with Ramon Ramirez. Ramon has been the president of Northwest Treeplanters and Farmworkers United (PCUN) since 1995. Many of my interviewees have referred to Ramon as the key leader who links together many Hispanic organizations around the state and nationally. He is chair of the Farmworkers Housing Development Corporation, is a member of 7 of the 10 organizations that form the CAPACES Leadership Institute, is president of the national Farmworkers Justice Fund and is on the board of three other national groups—Reform Immigration for America, Alliance for Citizenship, and the United Farmworkers Foundation.

I walk into the building that houses Ramon's office and find him seated at a desk in a tiny space, with papers and books stacked high, barely leaving room for a computer. He apologizes for the mess, due in part to the fact that he has no assistant to support his work. He has just gotten off the phone, confirming flight reservations for Montgomery, Alabama. He is headed there tomorrow, to participate in the anniversary of the march from Selma to Montgomery. He is very pleased that a major theme of the march has been dedicated to migrant workers.

As I listen to Ramon, I reflect on the words of a colleague. "Ramon tells his story from the eyes of justice, love and compassion."

I try to focus the discussion on his family and early life, in order to gain insight into how he has chosen the path he did, but Ramon quickly moves to the topic of civil rights.

In his early teens Ramon was inspired by the work of Cipriano Ferrel, who moved from California to Oregon in the mid-1970s and founded PCUN. The '70s was a time of repression of farmworkers around the country. President Nixon had implemented the Arthur Corwin Study, which warned that if we did not contain Mexican immigration, we would risk a separatist movement in the US. The term "illegal aliens" took hold during that time, and Nixon jailed many Chicano leaders.

Ramon was swept up in the immigration movement when his stepfather was stopped by immigration authorities and his sister's husband was picked up when his sister was six months pregnant. Ramon laments, "Our crime was crossing the border, but we are law-abiding people with strong families, opposed to drugs."

The conversation shifts back to Ramon's early life, where he participated in walkouts as a high school student. When he was a junior at an East Los Angeles High School, he heard Cesar Chavez talk about the need to go to college and then go back to the neighborhood. He inspired the students to believe that they were capable of taking action to change their circumstances.

After he left high school, Ramon started working with farmworkers. He moved to Oregon and attended Colegio Cesar Chavez with the goal of gaining the skills he would need to be a community organizer—communications, tv/radio production, photography, printing press, and silk screening. Before he was able to complete his degree, his passion for organizing drew him in.

There is fire in his eyes as he talks about the injustice that he sees all around him:

> *The 1986 immigration reform plan under Reagan did not deal with the root causes of immigration. We opposed the Reagan plan because it didn't go far enough. Because of the plan, 250,000 people in Oregon were waiting for green cards and 15,000 Oregon tree planters were excluded.*

Many of his coworkers were separated from members of their families:

> *Free trade is hurting Mexicans. The Mexican government used to buy local products. With free trade it is cheaper to buy US products. This puts Mexican growers out of business. And then they cross the border...*

When founder Cipriano Ferrel died in 1995, Ramon took

over as president of PCUN. The organization is involved with civil rights, immigrants' rights, and women's rights. Ramon's passion for leading PCUN stems to a large degree from his fear that anti-immigrant sentiment will have a devastating effect on Latino youth. He began working on the Dream Act in 1999, but he is concerned about the lack of progress: "The longer the promise of the Dream Act remains unfulfilled, the greater the hatred toward the US grows in young people."

Ramon was appalled when Attorney General Alberto Gonzales referred to border crossers as "terrorists," and when Bill O'Reilly said that if the 2007 immigration bill had passed, it would have been the end of the white male.

In 2007, Marcy Westerling from the Rural Organizing Project met with Ramon and the Farmworkers to develop a plan to debunk the messages of Gonzales and O'Reilly. They held over 100 "kitchen table discussions," each involving 5-20 people. According to Ramon, "These meetings planted the seeds for a movement."

With a strong leadership push from Ramon, 10 different Latino community organizations came together under the umbrella of the CAPACES Leadership Institute. They began meeting twice a month for training in leadership and fundraising. Every three months they organize a mass gathering of the 10 organizations. At each gathering, the group takes on a topic and then sets the topic for the next meeting.

Another group, called Clica, has formed out of these meetings. Clica is made up of academics and business partners around the state who share common goals with the 10 organizations. The president of the University of Oregon, as well as representatives from Costco and Bon Appetit, have participated, focusing on issues such as sustainability, pesticide safety, and labeling of products that are produced using equitable human rights standards.

As we wind down our interview, the anger in Ramon's voice fades and is replaced by hope. He tours me through the building, which had been built with $700,000 in funds raised from across the country. He is very proud of the fact that the CAPACES Leadership Institute now has a home to support leaders around the state who share his vision for Oregon's Latino community.

We end the interview driving by a farmworker housing project developed through the work of the Farmworkers Housing Development Corporation, where Ramon serves as president of the board. He talks about childcare, community gardens, and community activities that bring together farmworker families in an environment that reflects a world that Ramon has yearned for all his life.

Ramon has reason for optimism. The recent success of PCUN-related organizations in Oregon and pro-immigration efforts around the country has been extraordinary. In Oregon, a bill to provide driver's licenses to undocumented workers passed the Oregon legislature and promises to benefit up to 100,000 people. The tuition equity bill for immigrant students finally succeeded in the legislature after a 13-year battle. At the national level, immigration reform passed the Senate and is closer to reality than it has been for decades.

Ramon recoils, however, at the notion that this recent success has taken any of the the fire of militancy out of his belly. "Mellowed? Are you kidding? If anything, I have become more strategic in using tactics to get our message across and do successful organizing." He proceeds to recount a series of recent activities:

> *I led a rally and march to a labor contractor's home.*
> *I organized wildcat strikes of non-farmworkers.*
> *I was involved in three major lawsuits with Earth Justice.*
> *I led another suit against the EPA regarding the use of pesticides.*
> *I was arrested on Capitol Hill protesting for immigration reform legislation.*

Ramon Ramirez sets the bar high in his quest for a world of "respect, dignity and diversity." Talking with him, it is very clear that he is anything but satisfied. It is even more clear that the cause of social justice at the state and national level is moving forward in a powerful way as a result of his leadership.

Author's note: Five years after the interview, I caught up with Ramon. He was battling the recent changes in immigration policy that were having a chilling effect, both nationally and in his community of Woodburn. Yet he remained optimistic, based in the short term on recent legislative and legal successes and in the long term on his faith in a new generation of leaders who have developed skills in fundraising, organizing, social media, and political advocacy through the work of CAPACES and PCUN.

The Believer

"Every time I see a pregnant young girl, I think about the baby and the short straw it has drawn. That mother was a baby just a few years ago. When did public empathy for that baby change to anger and dislike?"

Rita Sullivan
September 2014

Sitting in the waiting area at the Medford offices of OnTrack Inc., I listen to the conversations in English and Spanish among four young men. They are laughing and telling stories. The conversation shifts to food stamps. One man asks whether another has a job yet. The answer is "no." A fragment of a conversation catches my attention. "…He came to the session loaded." The response: "That ain't no good."

Executive Director Rita Sullivan arrives and introduces herself to me. She opens by saying, "I've been in this seat for 35 years."

Rita was born in London, England and came to the US at age seven with her parents, brothers and twin sister. Her mother was a fashion designer who got her MFA from the University of London. Her father was one of 13 kids in a big, close-knit working class family. They owned fish and chips restaurants.

Because her mother repeatedly came down with pneumonia, the family sought a better climate in the US. They landed in New York and drove to Nebraska, where they had a family contact. Soon the family moved to southern California, where her father served as chef and manager for various restaurants.

Rita's father died in 1966, when she was 15. Rita married young and had a one-month-old baby when the 1971 earthquake drove her and her family out of southern California. They moved just across the Oregon border to Ashland, where Rita completed her BA and master's degrees. She later went on to get her PhD in San Diego.

She returned to southern Oregon in 1979 to do a doctoral internship at the Veterans Administration (VA) in White City, focusing her research on brainwave biofeedback (theta waves) as a means to treat addiction. Most of her work at the VA was with older chronic alcoholics, and Rita very much wanted to try this methodology on a different population.

She approached an organization called CARES (Center for Addiction, Rehabilitation and Educational Services) and was offered a job. During her time there, the director left. They hired a new director, but he did not work out and was soon fired. The board asked Rita to serve as director, as the agency was in a vulnerable state; but she balked. "I am a clinician. I don't know about administration."

She sought the advice of Carolyn Blanchard, then the director of Jackson County Health and Human Services, which CARES served as a subcontractor. She urged Rita to do it, offering to teach her what she needed to know. Rita reflects, "I said I would do it on a temporary basis. That was 35 years ago!"

As the program grew, the small agency called CARES changed its name to OnTrack, which now provides a full array of evidence-based model programs offering treatment, support, housing and related services to thousands of individuals and families yearly.

When people ask Rita if she will ever retire, she answers, "No. I will do this as long as I do it well. I love this work. You cannot get the turnaround with chronic mental illness that you can with addiction. People get well here every day."

Success has not always led to public recognition and funding. Rita laments:

> *Working with addiction has never been easy. The funding has been incredibly low and the skills required very high. Most of the funding has gone to mental health. People have not appreciated addiction treatment. But I have seen the evolution of this. We are now beginning to see the need to treat addiction, because it is implicated in virtually all of our domestic problems and drives our system of care.*

Reflecting on the victims of addiction whom she has served over the years, Rita shakes her head:

> *If I had been in the shoes of many of these people, I don't know how I would have survived. This is a motivator for me. If you are here at OnTrack, you are going to have people like me in your corner every day. I have a private practice as a psychologist, but my heart is in the public sector, where the*

problems are.

When she began this work, Rita was appalled by the fact that people who were having problems with addiction were not being helped. Instead, they were being shunned by society. From Rita's perspective, poverty is a huge part of the problem. "Many addicted people are like diamonds in the rough. They clean up very well." She says these words with the voice of experience and with great respect.

One of Rita's primary passions involves keeping kids with their biological parents. In 1989 OnTrack launched the Home Program. In 1990 she followed with the Dads Program. "Why should kids go to foster care just because the custodial parent is a male?"

These initial pilot efforts began her long-term commitment to family-based programs. "I don't think we can be effective without involving the entire family. In 1990, when I saw a baby removed from its family, I made a silent promise that I would devote my professional career to helping ensure that that does not have to happen."

In 2007, Jackson County formed a collaboration of partners committed to reducing foster care placements and making system changes that would result in better outcomes for children involved with the child welfare system. The partners included OnTrack, Jackson County's child welfare agency, Community Family Court, the Family Nurturing Center, CASA, Jackson County District Attorney, and Southern Oregon Public Defenders.

Advocacy

The selling point for this approach was based on hard numbers. National studies showed that two thirds of boys and half of girls who experienced foster care entered the delinquency system. By the age of 21, two thirds of girls had been pregnant more than once.

The collaboration is showing powerful results. The foster care placement rate for child welfare cases in Jackson County was cut in half between 2006 and 2011, while the statewide rate remained constant.

Armed with the success of this collaborative effort, Rita approached State Senator Alan Bates in 2011 and asked him if he would sponsor a bill that would help keep kids at home and not put them into foster care. Bates replied, based on his experience as a physician, "If the kids are in danger, you should lock the parents up!"

But Rita did not give up. She introduced Bates to judges, caseworkers, and other partners who worked with families involved with addiction. Armed with a new awareness of the problem, Bates introduced a Senate bill, the Strengthening, Preserving, and Reunifying Families Act, which was signed by the governor in 2012.

"Someone has to be a believer," Bates said. "Someone like Rita Sullivan has to have a strong vision and help people understand how valuable the program will be. Someone has to bring the parties to the table to work together."

Rita's most recent project is called Generations. It addresses the needs of two populations, which Rita refers to as the most poorly treated people in America: poor children and the poor elderly.

> *Seniors have a lifetime of knowledge that can be shared with families who don't have that life experience. At the same time, the main thing that makes seniors unwell is lack of purpose. I want every senior to have a purpose and everyone to have a family, a family of choice, even if the family of origin is broken.*

Recently, Rita was with a client and her child when the child said, "I am an OnTrack child, and I want to be a counselor when I grow up."

As she recalls this story, Rita talks about her staff. "About half of my staff is academically trained. The other half has been trained through experience (as former addicts). The best are both." Three of the members on her management team are people in recovery who have gone on to get their master's degrees.

"I have a stable core of staff. They are a skilled, committed group of people with an incredible gift of understanding. No one gets turned away from services here."

As we end the interview, Rita tells me a story about a visit to a local service club where she was seeking holiday gifts for families served by OnTrack. One club member emphatically stated, "I'll support presents for these kids, but don't give one penny to the drug-abusing mother."

"I was ready to confront him, but I held my temper and asked him, 'Is that 13-year-old mother a parent or a child?'"

As we end the interview, Rita repeats a theme which serves as her mantra, "You teach the parents and the kids together. That helps to break the generational cycle."

As I walk out, the young men in the waiting room have left, replaced by a group of young mothers and their infants. I think about the young men… the laughter… the teasing. Two hours before, I had tried to hide the judgment that I felt in my gut—losers, no future, a scary reflection on our society… Then I remember the words of one of the men: "That ain't cool." Someone was getting through to that young man. It was Rita Sullivan. After 35 years, her work is not done. For that young man, it is just beginning.

The Quiet Leader

> "Many of the people we serve are leading incredibly chaotic lives—in poverty, struggling with addiction or mental health issues. What we don't understand is that we're serving somebody's mom or child. We must figure out a way to help."
>
> Brenda Johnson
> May 2014

As I talked to others about nonprofit leaders to interview in Southern Oregon, Brenda Johnson's name came up frequently. She was described as an extraordinary leader—understated, strong, and gentle. One person described her as "very quiet in her leadership."

Our interview starts slowly. I learn that Brenda was born in Portland. She describes herself as very fortunate to have two incredibly loving and nurturing parents who taught her at an early age the importance of caring for one another. Her father was a business systems analyst and her mother a caregiver to four children. The family moved to St. Louis when Brenda was in second grade and then to Medford when she was 16.

I am becoming concerned that it might be difficult to get close enough to Brenda to discover what people or events in her life set her on the dramatic course of leadership that she has taken at La Clinica del Valle in Jackson County. But when I ask her about her friendships, she begins to relax. She talks about a close friend who had a big influence in her life, someone who was very kind and loving but experienced challenging mental health episodes that required her to be hospitalized various times while they were growing up.

"I recall the times very clearly, but I didn't understand what it was all about," reflects Brenda. "It was a very emotional time for me. My parents always said I was a kid who wore my heart on my sleeve. Instead of creating judgment, I wanted to deepen my understanding."

In her early twenties, Brenda did extensive research on what it is like to live with mental health issues. "This process helped me develop a greater understanding of what people go through."

Just after graduating from high school, Brenda attended Southern Oregon University (SOU) and Oregon Health and Sciences University in Ashland, eventually completing a double major in Spanish and nursing. While she was attending SOU, a Spanish teacher challenged her, asking her why she hadn't enrolled in an exchange program in Mexico. Brenda reflects:

> *I decided it was an exciting opportunity that I couldn't pass up. I was assigned to live with a family who spoke very little English. Even though I had taken several classes in Spanish, I knew I had a lot to learn. I ended up getting sick three months into the exchange.*

For Brenda, being in the vulnerable position of needing critical health care services in a foreign country without adequate language skills was terrifying:

> *I decided then and there that no one should have to feel that way. I am certain that experience had everything to do with why I chose to work for La Clinica. The same is true for many people who have come to the US, needing care in a language they don't fully understand. It's the same for them as it was for me in Mexico.*

Brenda returned to the US and worked at Baskin Robbins to pay her way through college at SOU. In her senior year she was recruited to work part time at La Clinica del Valle, a Medford-based health clinic serving a largely Latino population.

> *I was incredibly drawn to the nonprofit sector. The mission of La Clinica spoke to my heart. I was trained as a nurse and couldn't resist being connected to the community. I just knew it was the right thing to do.*

She worked at La Clinica for two years as a public health home-visiting nurse in a program that served mothers with new babies. She heard stories from women who had to go through incredible strife to find the American dream. Listening to all the abuses they suffered on their journey to the US taught her a lot about the resiliency of the human spirit.

Her next role at La Clinica involved writing grants and developing wellness and prevention services. She left La Clinica in 1998, but was recruited back at the end of 1999 to serve as deputy director. When the executive director took a job elsewhere, Brenda served as interim CEO while the board conducted a search.

The board hired Brenda in 2000, when she was 30 years old and pregnant. Brenda recalls:

> *I think the board took a risk on me because they understood the absolute passion I had, and still have, for serving this community. They appreciated the fact that I had experience as a nurse and that my time in Mexico had fundamentally changed who I am. I look back and feel honored that they saw strength in my commitment, my leadership and my deep passion for this work. They saw things in me that I didn't even see in myself at the age of 30.*

La Clinica started in 1989 as a program with 40 employees serving about 1,000 migrant seasonal farm workers, primarily pear and peach pickers. At that time Jackson County, Oregon was 4% Latino. Today, Latinos represent over 16% of the population, and La Clinica has 380 employees serving over 27,000 people per year. That's one out of every ten people in Jackson County!

Brenda's leadership derives from her experience and deeply held values:

> *I am personally driven to find equity in health for all people. I have been given the gift of experiencing first-hand how devastating mental health issues can be to people's lives. My challenge has been to learn how to take that experience and use it to support others. It is deep in my core. I am puzzled when I hear people complain about the work they do. My work is a gift to me.*

Advocacy

One of Brenda's greatest challenges is to maintain the rich culture of a nonprofit organization at a time of such rapid growth and expansion. She places a great deal of emphasis on new employee orientation, engagement and development. Every month she speaks to new employees about the history, culture and values of the organization.

Brenda's voice takes on a fierce tone when she speaks of her patients:

> *I remind staff that many of the people we serve are leading incredibly chaotic lives—in poverty, struggling with addiction or mental health issues. What we don't understand is that we're serving somebody's mom or child. We must figure out a way to help. We have a responsibility to care for one another. We go to the same parks, drive the same roads and see the same sky. People are experiencing pain and suffering. If I can do my part to help, I will!*

Brenda notes that at one point there was a waiting list of over 3,500 people for dental care. She went to the dental community to ask for help. "I rarely use anger to motivate. But when I thought about what those poor people were going through, I knew we had to do something about it."

La Clinica opened a 34-chair dental clinic in 2013. Today the number of people on the waiting list for dental services is zero.

Leadership of La Clinica has not always been an easy ride for Brenda. Four years after she took over as CEO, she received a "We the providers" letter from the physicians. It contained a long list of issues that were frustrating them. Brenda looks back on the lesson she learned that day:

> *My first reaction was total surprise. I felt this strange combination of feeling responsible and defensive at the same time. Looking back on that incident, I realize it was a gift. I was professionalized as a nurse to think about physicians in a particular way. And I was distancing myself from them. I learned that in order to be an effective leader, I had to go to much greater lengths to engage staff, to be honest and transparent, regardless of whether things were great or not so great. I learned that each time I would talk with our team members about an issue, they were the most directly connected to the best solution.*

Today, La Clinica has 38 medical providers (doctors, nurse practitioners, physician assistants, and midwives) and 15 dental providers (dentists and dental hygienists). One way they have been able to attract top talent is by helping young professionals work off their college loans. Others are leaving their private practices because they are attracted to La Clinica's rich culture and commitment to education. Brenda herself received her MBA from Purdue University in 2008, while employed at La Clinica.

Brenda is matter-of-fact:

> *Other nonprofits have struggled, but ours has grown at a time of severe economic changes. We believe that when we do the right thing, the resources follow. We make that connection real for people to understand.*

As Brenda looks to the future, she is optimistic. She sees the

Affordable Care Act as a great benefit for healthcare coverage for low-income people in Oregon. According to Brenda, health care reform, if organized well, has a chance of reducing healthcare costs and allowing for better coordination of care and services to the community as a whole.

> *In a small community, collaboration works! We just need to listen to the community and look beyond each organization's services to address the space in between, where some of the greatest gaps in services lie.*

Brenda Johnson's inner strength is not protected by a "no trespassing" sign. She seems to derive her strength through her openness to others—their suffering, their love, their willingness to join her in taking on the challenges that have shaped her career.

The people who recommended Brenda as a leader I should interview were right. Understated, strong, and gentle… I feel her strength as I drive away. And somehow the world seems to be a more hopeful place.

The Writer

"I've been fortunate. I decided I wasn't going to write the great American novel, but I could be around people who were writing great American novels and maybe get my two bits in."

Rich Wandschneider
November 2015

When I planned a trip to interview nonprofit leaders in the wide-open high desert and mountains of Eastern Oregon, the person I was most curious to meet was the founder of an institute for western writers who lives in the small town of Joseph, at the base of the Wallowa Mountains.

As I asked people about Rich Wandschneider, they advised me to schedule a good chunk of time, as Rich is quite a talker. I happily found that to be the case, but also found that his fascination lies in history, people and ideas—not in himself, and particularly not in his childhood.

Rich describes a Garrison Keillor-like upbringing in Fosston, Minnesota, with a German father and Norwegian mother. His maternal grandfather left Norway at age 16, and Rich's mother went to school speaking Norwegian.

Rich describes his father as a nerd, who went to school in Grand Rapids, Minnesota, where he washed dishes for room and board and in his spare time built radios. His family owned a restaurant and cream route. In his 30s, he worked in a Ford garage in Fosston, where he met and married Rich's mother. Later he worked for the post office. During World War II, Rich's father was transferred to the war department in Ogden, Utah, where he installed radios in airplanes. Meanwhile, Rich's mother took over at the post office.

Rich was born in 1942 and spent his first ten years in Fosston, where he played hockey in the winter and baseball in the summer. He proudly reports that he talked his way onto the junior high baseball team when he was in fifth grade. When his family moved to Oceanside, California in 1952, his sports career was temporarily interrupted. "I was pissed," he reflects. "I had just gotten a new pair of hockey skates."

In his new home, Rich got back into baseball. "I fell in with a group of boys who got good grades, played sports, and drank beer."

He wanted to go to Stanford, but when he didn't get in, he followed in the footsteps of his baseball coach and chose the University of Denver. After getting awards for his writing in high school, his first college paper was panned by his instructor, who advised him: "Wandschneider, cut out all those long, windy sentences and adjectives."

Rich transferred to the University of California Riverside and shifted his major from math to philosophy. Later he went to graduate school at Northwestern, but he was miserable in the

Midwest. "It was 1965 and the Vietnam War was just heating up. I applied and was accepted into the Peace Corps, leaving a record number of incompletes behind."

Rich began his Peace Corps career being dropped off in a village in eastern Turkey with a woman from Seattle. Many refugees from Bulgaria and Greece had moved there in the 1930s, and there were two Kurdish villages nearby. As a Peace Corps volunteer, Rich helped build a drinking fountain and community bathrooms.

After two years in Turkey, Rich returned to the US in 1967 and was in Washington, DC when Bobby Kennedy and Martin Luther King Jr. were killed in 1968. He participated in Dr. King's Poor People's Campaign, seeking donations from white suburban churches to support inner city DC communities. He continued his work with the Peace Corps, working at the Turkey desk and evaluating Iran's Peace Corps program.

After getting married in DC, he moved to eastern Oregon in 1971, where he worked for Oregon State University Extension in Enterprise with a cowboy who was a conservative World War II veteran. Despite their political differences, the two got along very well, establishing an employment office and a daycare center, as well as managing a Neighborhood Youth Corps project.

In 1976, Extension wanted Rich to move into land use planning and offered him jobs in Hood River and Ontario. Rich declined. Considering his options, he thought about the woman who had been his Peace Corps partner in Turkey. She had become a ski bum in Sun Valley and later went on to buy

Advocacy

a bookstore there. Rich talked her into coming to Oregon and helping him and his wife Judy open the Bookloft in Enterprise. The Bookloft became an incubator for the Wallowa Valley Arts Council, and they ran the operation from 1976 to 1988.

In the mid-1970s, Rich met a man who was to have profound effect on his life. Alvin Josephy was a renowned journalist and historian of the American West, who began with American Heritage magazine in 1960 and served as senior editor from 1976 to 1978. In the late 1970s, Josephy became involved with the Sun Valley Conference, which brought together artists and writers and other creative people. Rich thought, "We have to do that here!"

In 1986, an opportunity presented itself. Kim Stafford, a poet in Oregon, hosted a Northwest writers gathering at Lewis and Clark College in Portland. At the debrief session, Rich exclaimed, "This is not a Northwest writers gathering. This is an I-5 writers gathering." Stafford responded, "You're right. Why don't you host the next one in Wallowa County."

From that conversation, Fishtrap was born. The theme of the first Fishtrap in 1988 was "Western Writers, Eastern Publishers." Organized by Rich, Stafford, Alvin Josephy, and the Wallowa Valley Arts Council, attendees included Ursula Le Guin, George Venn from La Grande, Bill Kittridge from Montana, and Montana Indian writer Jim Welch.

According to Rich, "I didn't know a thing about putting together a writers' conference." Over 150 people paid $30 each to attend. Josephy recruited Naomi Bliven, a writer for The New Yorker, and Mark Jaffe, from Houghton Mifflin

Publishers, to be among the guests.

"We had a fine time," reflects Rich. "It was not about how to get your novel published. It was a revival meeting for writers."

Rich led Fishtrap for 20 years, from 1988 to 2008. During that time, thousands of people from all over the world met at Wallowa Lake for the annual summer gathering. Fishtrap also hosted Winter Fishtrap, writers' workshops, and The Big Read, when over 700 people in Wallowa County read *The Grapes of Wrath*.

The name Fishtrap originates from the Nez Perce word "wallowa," which means the anchor on each end of a trap designed to catch fish. Fishtrap's location, Wallowa County, was home of the Chief Joseph band of the Nez Perce tribe, on the edge of the Eagle Cap Wilderness, near the Snake River and Hell's Canyon. For Rich, the name symbolizes the program's local roots.

In 2006 Fishtrap hosted a meeting of Northwest foundations to discuss the future of the organization. Rich asked about the possibilities for endowments and larger capital campaigns. At that meeting, Cynthia Addams from the Collins Foundation commented, "You have to prove that the organization can survive its founder."

That comment got Rich to thinking. The opportunity to hand Fishtrap over to the next generation of leadership and pursue his many other interests motivated Rich to step down from his leadership of Fishtrap in 2008.

Advocacy

One of Rich's primary interests was to honor the legacy of Alvin Josephy. In 2003, a meeting was held in Portland involving library and literary figures from around the state to discuss possible locations for a library containing Josephy's works. Josephy wanted the library to be located in Wallowa County, given his deep-rooted connection to the Nez Perce and the American West. The response was that it was too remote, and the library idea was too expensive.

After Josephy's death in 2005, the decision was made to split his book collection between Wallowa County—in Fishtrap's basement—and the library at the Smithsonian's National Museum of the American Indian.

In 2010 a group of local artists and supporters conducted a feasibility study to determine whether an arts center could make it in Joseph. The answer was that it could, but not if it needed to retire debt. In 2012, Anne Stephens purchased a former bank with the idea that it could become an arts center. Rich became more involved with the group, and they formed a nonprofit dedicated to purchasing the building and naming it the Josephy Center for Arts and Culture.

The nonprofit currently rents the facility, with the understanding that they will buy it from Ms. Stephens at cost. Plans are underway to initiate a capital campaign to raise the necessary funds. The Josephy Library is housed in the building, and Rich serves as the library director, with Cheryl Coughlin serving as the center director.

In addition to the Josephy Center, Rich continues to give time to the Nez Perce Homeland Project, a cause to which he has devoted over twenty years. He writes a blog, to which "Ursula Le Guin will occasionally reply." He also teaches a class for Oregon State University at Eastern Oregon University in Le Grande, entitled Pacific Northwest Ecosystems and Tribes.

As we end the interview, Rich becomes philosophical:

> *The success of Fishtrap and the Josephy Center and Library were not accidental. You can't impose your own vision. You have to marry the idea and the place. There has to be a seedbed there. In Wallowa County we had ranchers who cared about the cause, the Nez Perce story, and Alvin Josephy.*

He concludes:

> *I have been fortunate. I decided that I was not going to write the great American novel, but I could be around people who were writing great American novels and maybe get my two bits in.*

As I drive along the road out of Joseph, looking up at the Wallowa Mountains, I reflect upon how fortunate Wallowa County and Oregon have been to have served as the home for Rich Wandschneider. Through his leadership in founding Fishtrap and supporting the development of the Josephy Center for Arts and Culture, this remote Oregon community, far from the I-5 corridor, is now a place where the arts thrive.

VI

A Later Calling

In all the interviews conducted for this book, I can't recall any individual who was motivated primarily by extrinsic rewards—salary or professional advancement. Each interviewee was motivated intrinsically in a manner that could be referred to as a calling. The stories in this chapter are about people whose calling came later in their careers. In each case, however, the delay in no way diminished the intensity of the calling.

The Tanzanian
Barry Childs was in the later stages of a successful corporate career when his homeland of Tanzania called him back to serve society in a completely different way.

The Orchestrator
Sharon Morgan was a homemaker and school volunteer on the Oregon Coast when an opportunity arose to take a job she

knew nothing about. Her decision to take a risk changed her life and transformed the arts in her community.

The Environmental Entrepreneur
Brad Chalfant's family had always expected him to become a successful attorney. He dutifully followed this pathway until a few meetings over beers with colleagues convinced him that he could devote his life to his first love—the land—and still make a living.

The Teacher
Debbie Vought had experienced first hand the trauma of growing up in a broken home. Although driven at an early age to take on leadership roles to improve her school and community, she drifted into an early marriage which failed and a career that fell short of her goals. Then the Columbine school shooting tragedy shocked her into embarking on a new cause.

The Black Pioneers
Willie Richardson and **Gwen Carr** are both African American women who grew up in the deep south and learned to succeed in business and government in predominantly white Salem, Oregon. When they retired, they teamed up to teach Oregonians about black culture and its contribution to the state.

The Tanzanian

"Reading the journal to others, and in particular the statement about making a commitment to something, was like taking a vow for me. Out of that experience came the gift [to me] of Africa Bridge."

Barry Childs
May 2012

Barry Childs grew up in Tanzania in the '40s and '50s. During the first 12 years of his life, he was homeschooled. He learned "the basics" from his parents.

The more colorful parts of his education came from several important people in his life. First, there was Colonel William Scupham (Colonel Billy to Barry), who witnessed Barry smoking his first cigar and drinking his first beer at age four. Then there was George, the great white hunter, who taught Barry how to swim in the river with crocodiles, a skill that later proved helpful in Barry's corporate role. Finally, there was Barry's father.

His father was a highly influential person in Barry's early life. His knowledge of agriculture and of village culture allowed him to take his skills as a botanist from agriculture extension work to the role of a provincial agricultural officer. He was a man who knew how to run with the foxes and hunt with the hounds. "He loved plants and parties," says Barry. In addition, he had a love for fast cars. As a young man in England, he used to race cars. In Tanzania, his work involved driving through the country for thousands of miles on rough dirt roads in a four-wheel-drive jeep.

"Back in those days," reflects Barry, "there were few people and plenty of prime land to go around. Today there are over seven times more people, limited prime land, and a lack of knowledge and capital to exploit the sub prime land."

At age 13, Barry left his rural home to attend his first formal classes at a Methodist boarding school in South Africa. He credits the school with contributing to his good values. These values were not always apparent on a day-to-day basis, however, and Barry admits that he was not a golden student. "I learned a lot about corporal punishment. But no matter how much they caned me, it did not diminish my free spirit."

Barry was very clear about what he wanted—to go to agriculture school and be a farmer. His father agreed, with one condition: "Go farm first. Then I'll help you go to college."

Nine months of farming resulted in a not so subtle change in direction for Barry. "It was hard work. I learned I wanted to become a 'gentleman farmer,' so I switched my degree to psychology and went to college in South Africa."

Once again Barry followed his father's lead, as he wavered between committed idealist and entrepreneurial schemer. On the one hand, he was part of a group of anti-apartheid activists who pressed their case for social and economic equality. On the other hand, he almost got thrown out of school with his antics as founder of the Dodo Night Club, created to bring life to a dull college town. "In the end Freud, Jung and Skinner kept me afloat," says Barry.

Barry's frustration with South Africa actually increased as his job opportunities flourished after college. He was benefiting from a system which he believed was, at its core, corrupt and unjust. The urge to see other shores inspired him to sell all his worldly goods and buy a one way airfare to London. During a trip through Europe in a "hippie wagon," he met a young woman, Hazel, whom he married on January 1, 1970.

Barry landed a job with Exxon UK in a sales role and remained there 17 years, rising to the role of head of training and development. He later joined Abbott Laboratories in Germany, where he served for 4 years, followed by an 11-year stint in Chicago. According to Barry:

> *I was always on the edge. Some managers didn't like me and were threatened by my role. The guys at the top were lonely and fearful—isolated due to their power. People were scared off by them and wouldn't be straight with them.*

As the year 2000 approached, Barry had become increasingly dissatisfied with his work. He was ready to move on. At a leadership conference in Chicago, a group of young African Americans confronted him and told him that his corporate stories were boring. Barry recollects, "They wanted me to tell them about Africa. I wasn't even aware that I had talked about

Africa!"

A young woman approached him and told him he must go to visit a missionary doctor in Tanzania. Barry contacted the doctor, and they stayed in touch. At one point the doctor invited him to visit. Barry offered to provide Total Quality Management training, and the doctor responded, "You've forgotten how to be an African. Come with no agenda."

In December 1998 Barry traveled to Arusha, Tanzania to visit the doctor's clinic. The land was beautiful and the people wonderful, but poverty and AIDS had devastated the town and surrounding villages.

One night Barry woke up at 3 a.m. and said, "I'm gonna do something!" At that moment he entered it into his journal. He read the journal to the doctor and his wife. When he returned home, he read it to Hazel and his children and friends.

> *Reading the journal to others, and in particular the statement about making a commitment to do something, was like taking a vow for me. Out of that experience came the gift [to me] of Africa Bridge.*

According to Barry, "The mission of Africa Bridge is about transformation—to transform the lives of the most vulnerable children in poverty-stricken villages of East Africa." But Africa Bridge goes further than simply these idealistic intentions. This transformation must be carried out by the communities and the guardians of the children themselves, not outsiders. Only then will the efforts be sustainable.

Barry used all his early education from his father in working with the local villages to train them to develop revenue producing agricultural crops through co-ops. The success of these co-ops, often run by women, provided the funds to support vulnerable children in their education. Local and regional governments were involved in and supported all the efforts.

Similarly, Barry used his corporate training skills in unique and creative ways. He engaged children aged 10-20, representing all the participating villages, in three-day Future Search planning sessions, where they described the lives they led, their aspirations and dreams and their ideas for change. Following these meetings, committees of community adults came together to do their own Future Search, where they developed plans guided by the hopes and visions for change of the youth.

As we conclude the interview, Barry tells me that he is facing the greatest challenges in his career and is working harder than he ever has. Since 2005, Africa Bridge has worked in 21 impoverished villages in rural Tanzania and served over 2,000 vulnerable households and over 4,500 vulnerable children, many who were orphaned and/or had AIDS. Forty-two village co-ops involving over 900 members are caring for vulnerable children, who are going from one meal a day to three meals, eating protein three times a week, not three times a year. Schools are growing and being built every year.

The success has been miraculous. And most importantly, the changes have been sustainable. Africa Bridge has been able to move on to new villages, as villages have become able to run these programs themselves.

At a time when most successful people are either retired or slowing down the pace of their careers, Barry Childs has found his calling and is fulfilling his vow.

The Orchestrator

> "Everyone wants to be a part of something larger than themselves. If you crack the door open and help them see themselves as part of it, it is wonderful."
>
> Sharon Morgan
> July 2010

As a child growing up in Everett, Washington, Sharon Morgan fondly remembers playing with her friends.

> *We created theatre sets in the open lots, parks and backyards and performed dances on the docks. Then we acted out dramas and movies, with the neighborhood as the stage. I directed the kids to play different parts.*

But childhood was not always play for Sharon, the only child of an Irish Catholic rancher and a mother whom Sharon refers to as a renegade, breaking from a conservative Dutch family. Her mother grew up in a remote part of South Dakota. Sharon tells a story of an eighth grade teacher who saw her mother's potential as a teacher and offered her a place to stay while attending normal school. Her father said "no." Oldest daughters were expected to help with the family. Discouraged, she quit before graduating from high school and married, helping her husband on the ranch and raising Sharon.

Refusing to resign herself and her young daughter to a lonely life on the ranch, Sharon's mother did something that was unthinkable in those days. She divorced Sharon's father, took her four-year-old daughter and moved west to Everett to open her own restaurant, using skills honed by cooking for the ranch crew.

The restaurant in Everett was a big success, staying open for the family-oriented dinner crowd to the 3 a.m. shift-change mill workers. Being the only child of a single working mother had its compensations. Customers made sure Sharon never missed a professional performance of the ballet, theatre and opera companies that played in Everett's civic auditorium, a WPA project built on the high school's campus.

A move to Moses Lake, Washington in Sharon's senior year of high school was a jolt that proved to be a happy experience. Without the stress of an after-school job, Sharon was able to make new friends and focus on academic challenges. Her mother was determined that Sharon not miss out on opportunities through education, as she had in her own life. With her support, Sharon blossomed academically. She attended Linfield College, in McMinnville, where she was a liberal arts major, with a strong emphasis on theatre.

She married her college sweetheart, Tom, right out of college and moved to Lincoln County on the Oregon Coast, where Tom's family owned a grocery store. As a young mother, Sharon was very devoted to her children. She wanted them to have rich educational experiences, especially in the arts. "I complained because there were not enough opportunities for kids. After a while I decided to stop complaining and do something about it."

She volunteered for four years in the schools, bringing exciting people into classrooms and taking kids out into the community. The schools decided to hire Sharon as a part-time employee, where she made learning come alive for many Lincoln County kids.

An opportunity came to her to take a job with the Oregon Coast Council for the Arts (OCCA), which had been founded five years earlier by poets in the community. The decision was a difficult one. Sharon knew nothing about running an arts council. At the same time she was determined not to follow her mother's pathway of missed opportunities.

> *I realized that an arts council was whatever I could conceive and get the money to support. I knew the community—its needs and its people. I wanted the arts to be a part of everything in the community.*

She knew that if she applied for the job, it would change her life. She did, and it did. At the time there was a building boom taking place on the coast. It made sense to Sharon to connect that activity to the arts, and she organized an event, "Contractors and Craftsmen," to bring these disparate groups together. The theme was artists working with architects and builders. She was inspired by the belief that "when you bring the visionary and the practical together, they beget wonderful children."

At the contractors and craftsmen event, the room was full of builders, architects, designers and artists. "You get people in the same room, and the energy flows. You have to trust that the magic will happen, even without you. Human beings are magic makers."

The meeting was a great success. Five business people, none of whom had ever considered getting involved in the arts, remain major contributors to this day. On that day the first seeds of a vision for a performing arts center were sewn.

Newport city manager Don Davis was the keynote speaker for the event. He had put together an urban renewal district and saw the possibility of building a performing arts center in that district. But there was a problem: the community had two theatre groups, and both refused to work together on the project.

With the help of Bob Kaul, a retired Minnesotan who was getting his master's degree in theatre from the University of Oregon, Sharon approached the two groups with a request. "Give us six months before you make a final decision whether to participate. At that point we will accept whatever you decide." The delay strategy worked.

Sharon knew she could get financial support from the National Endowment for the Arts (NEA), but she needed to get the community to support NEA as a partner and to raise a three-for-one match for NEA funding.

"I love these Machiavellian things," reflects Sharon, as she describes a visit to learn about the project by a Texan representing the NEA. "We hosted a lunch for him with community leaders. Before lunch was served, we hoisted the Texas and US flags. The luncheon was fabulous!"

For Sharon, bringing people together and creating a vision for a performing arts center in Lincoln County was the easy part. Also, getting the commitment of the major partners came quickly. The NEA stepped forward with a matching gift. The City of Newport agreed to use urban renewal dollars to fund the major costs of building the center, if the Oregon Coast Council for the Arts were successful in raising a $500,000 match.

Entering the fundraising arena, however, left Sharon with more questions than answers. She contemplated the challenge of raising $500,000 in a small community which had never done anything close to that for the arts in the past.

Although she had no experience in fundraising, she decided she needed to be audacious to achieve the goal. First she brought the Oregon Symphony to the coast. Later she saw an article in the paper about an Oregon philanthropist. She did her research, made a phone call, and set up a meeting with Norm Winningstad, founder of Floating Point Systems.

Winningstad was gruff and asked Sharon up front, "How much do you want?" After fumbling around for words, Sharon stuttered, "Uh, $500?"

"You got it!" replied Winningstad. Sharon learned a lesson. After that experience, she taught people, including herself, to look in the mirror and repeat again and again, "We need

$5,000!" Winningstad later gave $50,000, and his wife Dolores gave another $50,000.

With $100,000 in hand Sharon organized a series of lunches, warning her guests, "There will be an ask." Bob Kaul was the first to raise his hand with a $1,000 gift. Many gifts followed, and after six months, they had raised another $100,000. Those lunches launched a successful fundraising drive that eventually met the city of Newport's challenge and NEA matching requirement and set the stage for the construction of the performing arts center.

Between conception, planning, fundraising and groundbreaking, the Oregon Coast Performing Arts Center took five years to complete. Recently, the center celebrated its 25th anniversary.

Sharon continued to serve as the director of the Oregon Coast Council of the Arts until 2000, when she retired and moved to McMinnville. Since that time she has acted in community theatre, married her long-time soul mate Kathy Kollasch and enjoyed being a grandmother. She continues to be asked by schools, social service agencies and local governments around the state and country to help them think of ways to bring the community into the arts and the arts into the community.

As she reflects on her career, Sharon talks about an experience she had while doing a workshop for an arts council in New Mexico. Somebody asked the group a question, "Is there anything in the work you do today that resembles the play you did when you were a child?"

Sharon smiles and tells me, "When he asked that question, I started to laugh. I thought about the dramas we acted out as kids in Everett, Washington."

Sharon Morgan's life is a reminder that the person you were as a child remains with you for your entire life. Her role as a theatre director began on the docks and city parks of Everett and continues today, ten years after retiring as director of the Oregon Coast Council for the Arts. For Sharon, the stage was, and continues to be, the community; and the actors are the teachers, volunteers, business people and students who live there.

The Environmental Entrepreneur

> "This is the easiest place in the world to do what I do. Central Oregon attracts people who really want to get involved. They want to fish and golf and recreate, but they also want to give something back."
>
> Brad Chalfant
> February 2015

In selecting people to interview for this book, I typically rely on suggestions from people who know the community well. I've noticed a couple patterns that have emerged. First, it is rare to see a person nominated by everyone I ask. Second, the nonprofits that "save lives or change lives" most dramatically seem to get the highest profile.

Brad Chalfant's selection was an exception to both rules. Virtually everyone I talked to nominated him, and he represents one of the few individuals nominated who has done work with a natural resources organization. Furthermore, the comments I heard about him were that he is quiet and not really someone who stands out in a group.

On the afternoon we meet, I am struck by Brad's laid-back demeanor and dry, self-effacing wit. I have to work to move him off the subject of the Deschutes Land Trust and onto the subject of Brad Chalfant.

Brad was born in Colorado Springs. When he was six, he and his parents and younger brother moved to Kansas, where much of the family resided. But Brad never let go of Colorado, and he returned to the mountains each summer from the age of eight to eighteen, first as a camper and later as a staff member of Big Springs Camp, located in the Front Range of Colorado's Rocky Mountains.

He comes from a long line of attorneys on his father's side and automobile business people on his mother's side. He grew up expecting to go to law school and eventually end up in Colorado, but as he watched what development and sprawl were doing to the Front Range, he decided to look elsewhere. The lure of the Northwest, particularly exemplified by Governor Tom McCall, drew him to Oregon, where he enrolled in 1983 at Lewis and Clark's Northwest School of Law. He expected that he would practice environmental law.

But things didn't work out exactly as he planned. He reflects, "I realized after the first few days that I hated law, but I owed it to the family tradition to graduate from Lewis and Clark. I did more cycling, skiing and rowing than studying law."

Midway through his second year of law school, he started clerking for a small law firm, specializing in bankruptcies and foreclosures—but he hated that even more! In spite of that, Brad continued to work for the law firm after graduating and passing the bar.

One evening Brad had dinner with an old law school friend. They talked about their lives, their work, and what mattered to them. "Maybe it was inspiration, or perhaps a smooth bottle of scotch, but I gave notice to the firm the following day and soon left Portland to 'ski bum' in Bend."

After three seasons of ski-bumming, Brad applied for the assistant county counsel position with Deschutes County. He was not hired. From his perspective, he was lucky, as his heart was not in that job. But county counsel offered him a different position, managing the county's real estate. Instead of an office, he was given a pickup truck, a stack of maps, and a notebook of property inventories. Eventually the county commissioners realized they had an underutilized attorney as their land manager, and Brad's work became more office-bound and legally focused.

Brad loved many aspects of his county job, but small-town politics was not one of them. "A group of fellow county employees regularly got together for beers at Deschutes Brewery to share our thoughts, frustrations, and aspirations." The land use system was often a subject of the conversations. He continues:

> We saw properties lacking protection that needed it and protected properties that arguably didn't need it. In many ways it's a great system, but it inevitably polarized the community. There was a lot of frustration. We needed other solutions.

During one of these after-work beer sessions, Bruce White, who had beaten Brad out for the assistant county counsel job, suggested setting up a land trust, which, at the time, was only a vague notion to Brad. His imagination was immediately piqued, however, and the group began to explore the concept of a land trust for the Deschutes Basin. They put together a small group, which eventually became the nucleus of the board.

Nearly all of the group members were public employees, and they realized that they needed someone outside of government who might have more credibility with private landowners. Brad reached out to Win Francis, a local attorney who helped establish the High Desert Museum. In Brad's words, "He likes to start things."

They founded the Deschutes Land Trust in the fall of 1995 and received 501(c)(3) status in February 1996. For the first six to nine months, the trust was volunteer-driven, with only a part-time office manager to keep minutes at board meetings. Brad served as president. Following one board meeting, Brad and Win were having a beer. Win suggested, "If this thing is going to go, one of us is going to have to give up his day job."

> *Win knew that I had found my passion and he convinced the board to hire an executive director. Since the trust had no money, he committed to sweeten the offer and buy the beer as long as we were together.*

Brad took the job and began to develop a game plan for leading the trust:

> *I'm not the smartest guy in the room, but I've learned that the quickest path to success is to surround yourself with the smartest, most passionate people you can find. We try to be*

> *realistic and grounded and not promise more than we can deliver. We tend to think long term, about the big picture, while talking about the things that people care about. This is the easiest place in the world to do what I do. People come here in search of something, and you need to help them understand that it will take some work to protect it, but that they can make a difference. Central Oregon attracts people who really want to be involved. They want to fish and golf and recreate, but also they want to give something back.*

Brad talks with great passion about Camp Polk, a project that the trust has taken on. Camp Polk was set up in 1865 as a military garrison to protect travelers. When it became apparent that hostile Indians were not a problem, it was abandoned and later homesteaded in 1872. At the time the trust began working to acquire it, the owner had been subdividing it and was ready to sell the pieces.

This former wet meadow was once a salmon and steelhead spawning site, where Indians camped and collected roots. But the site had been cut off from its historic fish runs by the construction of three large dams downstream. It was further degraded following the Christmas of 1964 flood, when the Army Corps of Engineers encouraged local landowners to straighten and channelize the creek to reduce flooding. Residents who had arrived more recently were oblivious to the history of the meadow and its ecological value.

Brad goes on to describe in great detail the process by which the Deschutes Land Trust was able to purchase the property. First, the landowner was convinced to pull the property off the market. Then the trust turned to PGE, which was required to provide new mitigation for lost fish habitat due to the operation of the dam. Recognizing the growing pressure to preserve fish passage and improve upstream habitat, PGE agreed to help the trust buy the meadow. The negotiations to purchase the meadow took three years. At the same time, the trust worked with the Oregon Water Trust and the Upper Deschutes Watershed Council to restore the flow of the Whychus Creek, with funding support from the Deschutes River Conservancy. Brad reflects:

> *At the time, all these organizations were in their infancy, and the directors of each would frequently and informally meet over a beer to strategize or simply share information.*

Since the eventual restoration of Camp Polk Meadow would be an enormous undertaking, requiring effective communication, coordination and agreements among organizations that rarely collaborated, a real challenge loomed. Brad credits the Bonneville Environmental Foundation with playing a key role here in working with the Bend-based organizations, helping them break down barriers and work more collaboratively. According to Brad, "Small, young organizations don't always play well together, particularly when it comes to sharing funding and other limited resources."

The process was a slow one, eventually including the Crooked River Watershed Council, but was built upon a recognized need to approach watershed restoration holistically in order to create habitat needed to reintroduce historic runs of salmon and steelhead to the Upper Deschutes Basin. In this process, each partner brought its unique expertise, resources and relationships. Eventually, as the participants worked together, they learned to trust each other and relationships deepened. Today, the Deschutes Partnership is the most successful collaboration of its kind in Oregon, having received special recognition and funding from public agencies and foundations. According to Brad:

> *The Deschutes Partnership and the restoration of Whychus Creek are unique, but in many ways replicable, where you can get diverse parties to build trust and truly work collaboratively. Of course, it doesn't hurt to occasionally sit and drink a beer together either.*

Brad goes on to talk about other projects that involve acquisition of land for wildlife migration corridors as well as trails through previously inaccessible areas of beauty. "People who recreate here are often looking to get involved. Eventually we may see a trail from Sisters to the Deschutes as well as trails connecting Bend to Sisters."

Brad is particularly interested in reaching out to new residents and younger Central Oregonians:

> *The trust can go out and protect a lot of dirt, but if we don't connect to the next generation, it doesn't matter. If we can get families on the land—kids planting willows and releasing juvenile fish—then we can connect them to this place. It truly becomes their home.*

He elaborates on the daunting task of growing the trust:

> *We as an organization must grow to meet the needs of our communities. To do this we must embed ourselves into our*

A Later Calling

> *communities—Sisters, Prineville, Sunriver, LaPine, Bend, Redmond, Madras, Warm Springs, Grass Valley. We have a staff of ten and an operating budget of around $600,000. It's an incredibly talented and passionate group of people who work for peanuts, and they never cease to amaze me.*

Brad becomes philosophical as he looks to the future:

> *The trust is very selective about taking on new projects. I am concerned about what I leave to my successor in terms of future management of these lands. I want more than just a bunch of pin flags on a map; I want the map of our projects to tell a story that is truly relevant to the community and stands the test of time.*

It is well past 5 pm. Brad concludes in characteristically modest fashion, "If you can't do what I am doing here, you can't do it anywhere. I just have to stay out of people's way." At this point, I get up to leave, figuring that I better get out of Brad's way, so that he can join a group for some after-work project planning… over a beer.

The Teacher

> "I have always had a passion for kids who are struggling with the stressors that life and our culture put on them. It's only going to get worse until adults in our community rally and become invested in the lives of our kids."
>
> Debbie Vought
> June 2015

Education has always been a part of Debbie Vought's life. "I always heard that whisper through the trees."

That whisper began in her family with her maternal grandmother, who was born in England and received master's degrees from Sorbonne and Cornell before moving to North Jersey to teach. Her teaching career was cut short by the arrival of children. Her husband was a military man who worked for Hughes Aircraft and was the chief contract negotiator between Hughes and the organization that was to become NATO.

Later in life, Debbie's grandparents did a great deal of traveling and entertaining, rubbing shoulders with many wealthy people. Debbie was fascinated with this world. "That's when I became aware of philanthropy. Wealth is not intimidating to me. I know how to ask for money."

Debbie's paternal grandparents, Tennessee tobacco farmers, offer an interesting contrast. "Grandpa sold beauty products and Grandma worked in the Nashville Bible Bookstore to supplement their income."

Debbie's father was a rebellious teenager. He lied about his age to get into the Marines. "If he hadn't, he'd be like the kids I work with today—in jail." He calls his four years in the Marines the best years of his life prior to entering banking, where he spent the rest of his career.

Debbie reflects, "Dad had a soft spot in his heart for at-risk kids. While Mom's side of the family was highbrow and super well-educated, Dad's side was hardworking and passionate, almost to a fault."

Debbie's parents met through banking, as her mother served as a bank escrow officer. She was also an alcoholic, and Debbie lived with her aunt until the age of three, while her two younger sisters lived with their grandmother. "Mom had run out of family to watch us kids so she stayed home for a few years. She wasn't the stay at home type, though."

By the time Debbie was six, the family hired a Latino nanny so her mother could go back to work. "We were latchkey kids. With Mom's alcoholism and Dad's rebellion and at-risk childhood, I understood what family dysfunction is all about."

Debbie grew up in Lompoc in Southern California and spent her adolescent years in San Diego County. She vividly recalls one night when she was awakened to see a police car outside her bedroom window. A young teenager was being arrested and handcuffed. Her response was not one of fear, but of anger: "What could any child do that was so horrible that he had to be treated that way?"

Her compassion for troubled kids led her to activism at an early age. When she was nine years old, she asked her mother if she could "trick or treat" for UNICEF. She calls that "the beginning of my fundraising."

When Debbie was 12, her parents divorced. She felt lost, and school became her refuge. She was class president every year at high school, and raised money for numerous causes. Her sisters went a different route. "One of my sisters ran away at age 16 and had a baby. The other was involved with substance abuse. As the oldest I grew up pretty fast."

She often asked herself the question, "Does anyone care about me?" But she was fortunate to have several key mentors during her childhood years. Parents of a good friend would have her over for family dinners and take her on outings. She also recalls with fondness a teacher and a softball coach who reached out and made a difference. "I understood the power and value of caring adults in a kid's life."

Today, Debbie and her sisters are very close. One is an RN at a juvenile facility, and the other worked first as an escrow officer and more recently in the legal field.

Debbie always gravitated toward leadership. In 1979, during her senior year in high school, she was offered an appointment at the Naval Academy. That same summer, after senior year, she experienced a very meaningful trip to the Soviet Union. Later that summer she chose to turn down the Naval Academy and got married at age 19.

Immediately she realized that she had made a huge mistake and was overcome with remorse. She went back to community college and worked for a year. She reflects, "I loved school and wanted a premiere education." But unable to afford the top schools in the country, she attended UC San Diego, and as an undergraduate brought two boys into the world. A lover of books, particularly Russian literature, she became a literature major.

After graduating from college, Debbie wanted a divorce from a husband who was a philanderer and suffered from an undiagnosed mental illness. "I knew I would be a single mom. I wondered how I could apply my passion and still have time for kids. I decided I wanted to teach."

In 1988 Debbie divorced her husband and was hired to teach English in the town of Temecula, just north of San Diego. She loved her work and remained there for eight years. In 1996 she went to Cal State Sacramento to get her master's degree, majoring in writing. She had been dating a Marine captain, who was stationed in San Diego. They got married in spring of 1997. In spite of finishing all the necessary coursework, Debbie never returned to get her master's degree, due to a scheduling requirement that would have conflicted with her wedding date.

After leaving the Marines, her husband had moved to Klamath Falls to get his engineering degree at Oregon Institute of Technology. Debbie left her teaching job and followed him to Klamath Falls in 1997, where she secured a teaching job.

As an Oregon teacher, Debbie could not ignore the growing problem of school violence. The 1998 shooting in Springfield, Oregon was especially close to home and painful:

> *I have always had a passion for kids who are struggling. I couldn't get out from under the weighty concern for kids. Too many kids came to my class not ready to learn, often due to stressors like bullying, poverty or challenges at home. It's only going to get worse until adults in our community rally and become invested in the lives of our kids.*

Debbie describes a "tsunami of feeling" that she didn't act upon until Columbine. "Columbine shocked me. It became clear to me that I really wanted to do something. But I needed a champion."

At the time there were no one-to-one mentoring programs in Klamath Falls. She started knocking on doors. "I drew blanks from the mayor, the superintendent and others. They were not willing to step forward. Then somebody said, 'You should talk with District Attorney Ed Caleb.'"

Debbie describes Ed Caleb as 6'5", with "Clint Eastwood good looks" and a booming voice. "Ed was trying to get parents together after Columbine. I tracked him down, and we talked for two hours."

Ed soon realized that he had a valuable partner in Debbie Vought. He offered her an office and support from his paralegal. His message to Debbie was simple: "I have a meeting coming up with parents. Tell them!"

The parents loved Debbie's message, and the idea for Citizens for Safe Schools (CFSS) was born in the aftermath of that parent meeting.

We didn't want metal detectors, zero tolerance, and armed teachers. We wanted to focus on prevention and talk about respect. I felt I had to take a militaristic approach. First mobilize the troops and then fight on different fronts—law enforcement, parents, educators.

In 1999 CFSS was formally created. Although she was very active, Debbie still taught until 2001, when she reduced her teaching to part time and then dropped teaching altogether to devote her full energy to CFSS. She gives a great deal of credit to Ed Caleb for the creation of CFSS. "Ed was the ordained authority. He empowered me. He opened doors."

Debbie's hard work and commitment to the cause is supported by strong philosophical principles. "What people need early and often in any movement is inspiration. People need to believe in the cause. This organization is about one-to-one mentors for high-risk kids."

In the sixteen years since its creation, CFSS has made a huge difference for at-risk youth and families in Klamath Falls. Every year 75-110 mentors each work with the area's most at-risk children, representing over 100,000 volunteer hours since program inception. Research studies have shown that participants are three times less likely to commit an act of delinquency. Almost 70% have improved their academic performance and close to 80% have made overall improvements at school. Furthermore, 85-95% of participants sustain their gains after one year.

But for Debbie Vought, the success of CFSS is about individual lives that have been changed. She describes a scene that had just taken place several days earlier. She was talking with a school principal and social service worker, focusing on the 168 kids who were on the "at-risk" list. The name of a young man who had been given a CFSS mentor a year before came up. No one from his family had graduated from high school. One of his family members was incarcerated. He had only one pair of shoes. The principal suggested taking the young man off the list, as he was doing well in school and his attendance was up above 90%. Debbie later met with the young man and told him, "I just heard someone bragging about you." According to Debbie, "He beamed from ear to ear."

Another young girl talked about how much her mentor meant to her: "I was in a dark place before I met my mentor. My younger brother was autistic, and nobody paid attention to me. I had dreams of becoming a veterinarian and was going to give it up. But my mentor wouldn't let me."

According to Debbie, "I've been around teens all my life. I know how dark those places can feel."

After we conclude the interview, I reflect on how Debbie Vought struggled with darkness in her own life. But instead of submitting, she learned from her experience and devoted her life to teaching others how to escape into the light.

The Black Pioneers

"If you respect yourself, you can respect somebody else, even if they are different. You become an educator every day in teachable moments."

Willie Richardson
July 2015

"The gift you give people is information. It gives black people pride in being part of the state."

Gwen Carr
July 2015

The only interview from this book that involves more than one interviewee takes place in a small office above Pioneer Trust Bank on Commercial Street in downtown Salem, Oregon. The two women who lead the all-volunteer organization, Oregon Black Pioneers, have a rich story to tell.

Willie Richardson left her native South Carolina 37 years ago to come to Salem, Oregon, but she never lost her southern roots. According to Willie:

> *South Carolina gave me my values and my belief in myself. I came from a traditional African-American community, where a community raised its children. When I came to*

A Later Calling

> *Oregon in 1978, the only black people I saw were my family and three sisters. That was a shocker, coming from a background where the only white people I knew were employees and coworkers in a factory environment.*

Willie credits her deeply-instilled values and grounded sense of self with her ability to adjust to this new and different environment. "If you respect yourself, you can respect somebody else, even if they are different. You become an educator every day in teachable moments."

When Willie was six, her father, who worked for the highway department, was killed in a work-related accident. Her mother moved to Philadelphia, but did not want to raise her kids in the big city. Willie, the eldest of five girls, was raised by her grandparents in the little town of Westville, about 20 miles west of Camden, South Carolina.

"My grandmother was the most influential person in my life. I never saw her not smile. She still talks to me, even though she has been dead for years." Willie's grandfather worked for a heating company and did a little farming to feed the family. Neither grandparent had gone to school beyond third grade, but education was important to them, and they encouraged Willie and her siblings and aunts to get a high school education.

Willie's grandmother would cook for her church for special gatherings, preparing food all week and sometimes feeding over two hundred people on Sunday afternoon. She repeatedly told Willie, "Cooking is my talent. You need to recognize what your talent is." In those days small churches would host events together to support each other in raising money for church projects such as putting on a new roof. According to Willie, the practice still happens today in some rural areas in southern black communities.

Willie attended segregated schools which served black students within a 50-mile radius. They were bused from all directions and would pass one or more white schools on their long bus rides. Willie has fond memories of her teachers. "What you knew, without a doubt, is that they loved and cared for you and would do everything they could to prepare you for life and the workforce."

Willie got married soon after she graduated from high school and had three babies. Today her two daughters are educators. Her son, after 20 years of service, is a retired Air Force sergeant. And Willie happily reports that she is still married to her high school sweetheart, Thomas.

When Willie turned 30, the husband of one of her sisters was accepted to Willamette University. They moved to Salem and convinced another sister, who lived in Philadelphia, to follow. Willie and her family at the time were living in Lugoff, South Carolina, and were also considering a move. In August 1978, they made their decision and completed the move to Salem in November. Willie reflects:

> *The move was a shock. If I hadn't run out of money, I would have packed up and gone back to South Carolina. Except for my family, I didn't see anyone else in Salem who was black.*

Because she felt out of place in this different culture, she was careful only to venture out in the community when accompanied by her sisters. But one Saturday she went out alone with her kids to the Lancaster Mall. The girls were 11 and 12 and the boy was two. They were very cute, and people would stop and admire them. But for Willie, the reality that they were the only black people in the mall hit her very hard. "I panicked and said to myself, 'I've got to get my babies out of here.' I got them into the car as quick as I could and took them home."

For the next several weeks Willie was too terrified to go out and only left the apartment to go to work at her state job. At that point she had to make a decision—either stay and figure out how to live or leave. "I chose to figure out how to live."

Living in an apartment was not to Willie's liking, so she and Thomas decided to buy a house. Her first experience was a bad one; the realtor introduced her to the owner of the house they wanted to buy, and soon after the sale was called off. But they did not give up and eventually bought a house in South Salem.

For the first few months it was a cold and lonely winter. When the weather warmed up in May, Willie was determined to meet her neighbors, primarily to make sure her kids would be safe in the neighborhood. She went from house to house within a three-block area and invited her neighbors to a picnic at her house. To her delight, they all came! Many had lived on the same block and never met each other.

> *That's when people started to be more friendly to each other and not just curious about their new black neighbors. After that picnic we realized that we were all good people and*

needed to watch out for each other.

Later, Willie branched out beyond her neighborhood and began attending school board and city council meetings, leading to her election in 1987 to the Salem School Board.

After 14 years working for the state, Willie opened up a business: Willie's Fashion Hats and More. She later moved downtown, and the hat shop evolved into a second business, A Time for Elegance.

Willie met Gwen Carr in 1981. According to Willie, "We've been kicking it together since then." I turn to Gwen and ask her to tell her story.

Gwen Carr was born in Los Angeles. Like Willie, her mother took her to a small town to live with her grandparents. In Gwen's case, that small town was Centerville, Texas. Her grandfather was a sharecropper, and her grandmother was a dedicated churchgoer who believed in living a disciplined life. She had attended a Methodist-supported college for two years and taught for several years, but according to Gwen, "She was always a teacher."

Gwen's family lived in a segregated community about a mile down the road from Centerville, and she attended a black-only school. Gwen reflects that having separate schools was odd, given how tiny Centerville was. In spite of some difficult experiences growing up (Gwen recalls feeling "less than" others), her grandmother always reminded her, "You are as good as anybody and better than most." Her grandmother's encouragement, along with her experience making public presentations in church, helped Gwen overcome her insecurity and develop confidence in herself.

Back in LA, Gwen's mother met a man who was born in South Carolina and grew up in New York. After World War II, he left New York to seek work as an airline mechanic in LA. When they got married, an enthusiastic seven-year-old Gwen moved to an ethnically diverse community in East LA to live with them. Later they moved to Compton, and Gwen attended Centennial High School, where the student body was 90% black. Gwen remembers only two white girls in the entire school. Like Willie, Gwen had a positive school experience. The black teachers (about half) were dedicated to educating black children, and the white teachers were idealistic and wanted to teach in the inner city. Gwen remembers:

> *The teachers taught us to be competitive because they understood the challenge that lay before us—to survive in a world that still saw black people as inferior. Their message to us was: "You don't have to be as-good-as; you have to be better-than."*

After graduating from high school, Gwen enrolled at California Lutheran College. "I got caught up in protest, and my discipline for study went out the window." Gwen's mother feared that her "natural" hair would identify her as a radical. For Gwen it was a source of pride. Later Gwen transferred to Long Beach State College, where a friend convinced her to get into law enforcement. "I applied for a position as a deputy with the LA County Sheriff's Department. To my surprise, they took me. I did it for a couple of years. It wasn't me, but I learned a lot."

A Later Calling

After Gwen left law enforcement, she got married and worked for two LA insurance companies. She was not unhappy in LA but would often reminisce about an experience she had as a girl scout in Coeur d'Alene, Idaho. "We did a lot of camping. It set a vision for where I wanted to be as an adult."

When she traveled to Oregon on business, it reminded her of Coeur d'Alene. "I didn't want to wait until I was too old to get out of the big city. I thought, 'Let's try Oregon!' "

Her husband found a job in accounting for a company in Portland. After being on the rise in management in LA, Gwen struggled to find a job in Oregon. "I was surprised how backward Oregon businesses were." She finally landed a job at the State Accident Insurance Fund (SAIF) as a project manager in information systems.

For 25 years, Gwen worked for SAIF and was actively involved in the National Association for the Advancement of Colored People (NAACP). She retired from SAIF in 2003. When Willie heard that Gwen had retired, she invited her to get involved with Oregon Black Pioneers. She felt that Gwen's project management and public speaking skills were well suited for the challenge. Gwen didn't hesitate. She reflects, "We had been hanging out with each other for a long time."

Our conversation turns to Oregon Black Pioneers, founded in 1983 by Salem-Keizer School's deputy superintendent, Carol Davis, State Senator Jackie Winters and David Burgess. After only a few years, the organization became inactive. Despite her interest in Oregon Black Pioneers, Willie's business didn't allow her time to get as involved as she wanted.

By 2004 Willie's business had become less demanding, and she felt a strong calling to serve Oregon Black Pioneers. She had a clear vision of how the organization could bring to life Oregon's African-American history and contribution to the state. She reflects, "My passion for Oregon Black Pioneers comes from the lack of knowledge and awareness of black history in Oregon."

She called Senator Winters and asked if she could have the organization turned over to her. Willie was given the green light. Oregon Black Pioneers became her first love, and she fully retired from her business in 2010 to devote more time to the organization.

Today Willie and Gwen work together as volunteers to bring black history to the entire state of Oregon. According to Willie:

> *Telling the story and telling the truth about the story is important for history. Much of our information comes from white people or historical societies, because they have the diaries, newspapers, obituaries, and other documents which contain important information. People are sometimes fearful about sharing the information, but we are clear that we just want to tell the story and don't want to beat you up for what your grandfather did. That makes it easier. They become part of sharing Oregon's African-American story.*

They are a good team. In Willie's words, "What Gwen does, I cannot do—research. I am a people person. I work with people and help them find the little bit they can do to help." Gwen adds:

> *History comes alive with stories which make me curious to do the research. It's like a puzzle. You find bits and pieces That leads to something else. The gift you give people is information. It gives black people pride in being part of the state.*

Willie agrees:

> *These stories demand to be told. They are important to the fabric of the state. I tell my grandchildren, "History should be important to you. We are here because somebody along the way paid a price."*

When Oregon Black Pioneers was launched in 1993, they gave out scholarships and had an annual gala celebrating black history in Oregon. When Willie and Gwen got involved, they began researching Oregon's black history in earnest. After six months, they realized the immensity of their project and narrowed their focus to Marion and Polk Counties. That took two years!

Since that time they have accomplished a great deal. From February until June 2015, the Oregon Black Pioneers featured their third exhibit on black history at the Oregon Historical Society. *A Community on the Move* told the story of how World War II shipyards, migration from the south, the Vanport flood, and urban renewal impacted Portland's black families and businesses in the 1940s and '50s.

After interviewing Willie and Gwen, I attended the exhibition and was amazed by the extent and quality of the research and visual storytelling. I marveled at how such a product could be produced by an organization of volunteers. When I call Willie to tell her of my experience, I can feel her smile over the phone:

> *This thing is pulling us along. People want to do and hear more. I envision this organization bringing about a change in perception. Without this story, Oregon's story is incomplete. When your life places you in a bowl and you don't venture out, that is your doing. Our job is to get you the information to get you out of that bowl.*

With vision, drive and enthusiasm, Willie and Gwen continue to get many Oregonians "out of that bowl." As Willie says, "History can be painful." But over time it will make us a more tolerant and enlightened people, thanks to the efforts of Oregon Black Pioneers Willie Richardson and Gwen Carr.

VII

New Approaches to Leadership

For most successful nonprofit leaders, there is a purpose that drives their passion. It could be be homelessness, the arts, domestic violence or any number of worthy causes. Chapter 7 focuses on four leaders who certainly are inspired by a cause, or "what" they do, but whose new approaches to leadership also reflect a passion for "how" they do it.

The Newcomer
Roberto Jimenez, after spending much of his youth traveling and exploring other cultures, was drawn back to his roots to pursue a leadership role in the Latino community. In doing so, he challenged the status quo and pushed leaders to achieve the same goals by collaborating with the banks, being more pragmatic and focusing on the bottom line.

The Salvage Entrepreneur
Terry McDonald inherited leadership of a traditional St. Vincent de Paul in Lane County from his father. He then turned it into a major entrepreneurial enterprise, with over 500 employees and a $25 million budget, developing new products and expanding markets without compromising the social justice mission upon which St. Vincent de Paul was founded.

The Pragmatic Idealist
As she was growing up, **Swati Adarkar's** visits to her parents' native India inspired her strong values relative to social justice, equity and opportunity. Her early experience with nonprofits led her to believe that the sector needed a tougher approach—a commitment to results and accountability and stronger alliances with the private sector. Her ability to blend compassion with hard-nosed pragmatism produced results.

The Traveling Teacher
After dreaming of being an actor as a child, **Bill Rauch** realized that his place in theatre was as a director. His passion to engage the community led him to travel across the country, recruiting people off the street to be actors in his plays. Later, following Shakespeare's lead, he used our country's history to shed light on our lives today. Bill Rauch brought the real world to theatre. As the two met, both were dramatically changed.

The Newcomer

> "You must collaborate, compromise, be pragmatic and look at the bottom line. If you can balance mission and the bottom line, you can be a leader in the community."
>
> Roberto Jimenez
> July 2012

I first heard about Roberto Jimenez's work in housing in the community of Woodburn from his father, Eli Jimenez. Eli is part Apache and Spanish and grew up working the fields with his parents as a migrant farmworker before walking off the job at age 14 and wandering into town. There, he talked the owner of a restaurant into hiring him, which began his journey as a successful high school and college graduate, a high school science teacher for many years, and, after retirement, an artist and lifelong learner whose youthful spirit belies his nearly nine decades of living.

As I mentioned, Eli had spoken glowingly about his son's work in housing. But when Ramon Ramirez, President of the Northwest Farmworkers Union, enthusiastically described to me the work Roberto does with the Farmworker Housing Development Corporation, I realized that Eli's words represented more than just paternal pride.

Roberto Jimenez was born in Oregon City, the youngest of five siblings. His three oldest siblings all left after high school because growing up in Oregon City was difficult for them. They would often ask him, "Why did you stay?" Roberto explains:

> My siblings grew up in the '60s. I grew up in the '70s. The baby boomers are more idealistic. We grew up in more pragmatic times—the gas crisis, the Vietnam War, the Weather Underground. I was very politically aware at a young age.

Roberto graduated from Oregon City High School in 1981, in the midst of a terrible recession. "The paper mill used to employ 25,000. When I graduated, the number was 2,500. The kids of loggers and millworkers were not prepared to do anything else." Roberto remembers his family life:

> When I was growing up, we had family meetings. I was expected to come to the table with a point of view. There was a huge expectation from my parents: You will educate yourself. You will work hard, do your chores and do good work. And you will value your community and give back to your community.

By the time his older siblings went to college, there was no money left for Roberto's education. His response was to work in restaurants and travel for ten years.

A visit to Istanbul changed his life. The night he arrived, there was a bombing at a synagogue which served Sephardic Jews who had migrated from Spain. The Sephardic Jews had lived there in relative peace for 500 years.

The culture of Istanbul fascinated Roberto, who got a job at a hotel and remained there from 1985 to 1989. Learning Turkish was his first challenge. As a non-European language, he could not simply translate words, but had to learn to think in Turkish. There were other challenges. The poverty and economic and political upheaval hit close to home. When the economy tanked and inflation reached 100%, Roberto realized that it might be years before he had the freedom to come and go. "I realized that to have the impact I wanted in the world, I needed to pursue further education in my own country. In Turkey I had no standing."

In the summer of 1989 he returned home and went to Portland Community College, financing his education by working in Portland restaurants. It was a very political time, and he befriended artists and musicians. He finished his degree in comparative literature at the University of Oregon. "After Turkey, this was my second life-changing experience. It taught me how to think."

After graduating, Roberto returned to Portland, where he was hired as a corporate trainer, teaching English. In 1999 the company went offshore, and Roberto was at a crossroads. Oregon was a different place than it was in the early '80s. Immigration from the south was having an impact, and many restaurant jobs, formerly filled by white working class employees, were now held by Latino immigrants. For Roberto, this presented an opportunity:

As I got to know these people, I realized that they didn't have the skills to integrate into the culture. That intrigued me, based on my study of culture through comparative literature. Also, I come from a long line of teachers and preachers. My family has always been activist and politically involved. It became clear to me that I wanted a leadership role working with Spanish-speaking people.

Roberto took advantage of this opportunity to do a best-practices study of Latino microenterprises in Hillsboro. This led him to apply for a job as executive director of the Farmworker Housing Development Corporation (FHDC) in Woodburn. FHDC was founded in 1990 and represented a partnership of five community-based organizations. Ramon Ramirez, President of PCUN (Pacific Northwest Farmworkers and Treeplanters Union), had been chair of the board for 19 years.

The hiring process was intense. Roberto went through five interviews, with the final interview involving 13 people. They finally hired him. A friend and colleague later asked him how he had the nerve to apply for this position in spite of having no development or executive experience. "I still don't know how to respond to that," Roberto tells me. "It was a grueling learning curve."

After several years at FHDC, Roberto participated in a program at Harvard's Kennedy School of Government called Achieving Excellence in Community Development. This third major life-changing experience gave him the confidence to challenge the status quo and move the FHDC organization into areas where his board was not initially prepared to go.

> *At the FHDC, we are real estate developers, property managers, educators and investors. We work very closely with banks—a conservative crowd. We needed to streamline our operation and abolish our membership-based organization.*

He goes on to describe the process of abolishing membership at FHDC. There was a great deal of heated debate. The chair of the board challenged the changes Roberto was suggesting, asking, "Are we going to let these bankers tell us how to run our business?"

Roberto responded, "We've been in bed with the banks for years. We either do this or get out of housing. It's worth it."

The debate went on for months, but they ultimately followed Roberto's lead, making the final decision an hour before Roberto graduated from the Harvard program.

During our interview, Roberto gives me a tour of the Farmworker Housing Project in Woodburn, where his office is located. It is very impressive, incorporating not only housing, but a preschool education center, community gardens, and other community facilities. The houses are well maintained, the gardens green and productive, and the people well-dressed and very friendly.

The project began as a senior housing project that stalled during the recession in the late 1980s. When FDHC applied to take over the project in the early '90s and sought funding to support housing for farmworkers, they were met with stiff resistance. The federal funders were reluctant to earmark money for a project that represented a special interest group—

in this case, farmworkers. The civic leaders in Woodburn were not supportive.

FHDC was running out of options when they went directly to then-Governor Barbara Roberts, who interceded with the local government and the federal funders on behalf of the FHDC. With Governor Roberts' help, the FHDC prevailed; the state's first farmworker housing project was born. To this day Barbara Roberts refers to this as her proudest moment as governor of Oregon.

Leadership of the FHDC has not been easy. Roberto has had to make some tough choices, including staff reductions, to keep FHDC alive during the most recent recession and its aftermath. Even though Oregon's economy is in recovery, many of the middle-class jobs have not returned. For many Oregonians the percentage of a worker's income that goes to rent or housing has risen from 25% to 30%. Funding for organizations like FHDC is not increasing, and they are increasingly diversifying and consolidating.

Roberto feels that FHDC must change to reach its goal of expanding opportunities for affordable housing to northwest farmworkers. He is pressing his board to take on the role of property management for other housing projects. "We are unique in that we are Spanish-speaking and culturally aware of the Latino and rural populations we serve. For-profits focus on the bottom line, but we bring more value."

Roberto looks to the future:

> *We have a 10-year plan to own and/or manage 1,000*

units of housing by 2021. This would allow us to earn enough income that our organization would become self-sufficient. We've gone from under 200 units in 2012 to 275 today. We have six years to figure out how to build another 700.

Again, Roberto is finding resistance from his board to the idea of moving ahead so aggressively. They want to move ahead with the model, but insist on controlling the program. Roberto feels that a property management company must be created, with some independence from the FHDC board.

Rather than backing down, Roberto is preparing to push his ambitious plan. A colleague describes Roberto as "fearless but not reckless. I don't know of any other executive director who will shake his organization like a snow globe and then stand back and honestly evaluate what he sees."

After our tour, Roberto describes the last lecture he attended at Harvard. According to the lecturer, the private sector alone cannot innovate in a way that will bring broad benefit to the community. There is too much emphasis on the bottom line. At the same time, the public sector working alone lacks the resources and the entrepreneurial motivation. The best results come when strong nonprofits collaborate with the public sector and with business. It is these partenerships that will inovate and save the country.

Roberto summarizes what this message means to him: "You must collaborate, compromise, be pragmatic and look at the bottom line. If you can balance mission and bottom line, you can be a leader in the community."

As Roberto Jimenez prepares his strategy to gain board support for launching the property management operation, his situation reflects the difficulty for nonprofit leaders who take on the challenge of the Harvard lecturer to "innovate and save the country." Surely, this will be Roberto's fourth life-changing experience. I wish him well!

Author's note:
In July of 2016, the tension between Roberto's push for change and the board's resistance came to an end, and Roberto parted ways with FHDC. According to Roberto, "I am enjoying not being in a leadership position. Whether I continue to not be in leadership, I don't know. Time will tell." As the author of this story, my guess is that it won't be long.

New Approaches to Leadership

The Salvage Entrepreneur

> "Either you go out of business or find a different answer. My way to survive was to go to the dump."
>
> Terry McDonald
> April 2014

I arrive early at St. Vincent de Paul in Eugene for my interview with Executive Director Terry McDonald. Since I have some time, I visit the retail store. The facility itself is impressive, and the merchandise on the shelves catches my attention. My 15 minutes melt away quickly, and I still regret not having time to pick up some books on tape, kitchenware, and at least check out the furniture.

Several people have told me that Terry McDonald is a person I must see in Eugene. My level of curiosity is very high as I walk up the stairway to Terry's office, passing a graphic timeline drawn on the wall, starting back in the mid-1900s.

Initially, Terry doesn't strike me as an extraordinary guy, either in appearance or conversation, as he reels off dates in order to give me a history of the agency. I note that this is a guy who is into timelines! I finally interrupt him and ask him to tell me about his early life.

Terry's mother was born in Portland and moved to Seattle in the early 1930s, where she became a top women's tennis player. His father was also a tennis player. Just before World War II they moved to Bremerton, Washington and bought a bowling alley. Even though it was a successful business, they picked up stakes and moved to Roseburg, Oregon after the war, where they raised five kids and purchased an ice cream parlor. Terry was the youngest. Two of the children had polio.

In 1951, two years after Terry was born, his father went into real estate. Several years later, Father E.J. Murnane of the local Catholic parish enlisted his father's help in starting what Terry refers to as a "salvage bureau." It was incorporated in 1955 as a St. Vincent de Paul thrift store. Terry's father served as its first director from 1955 to 1984.

Much to my surprise, Terry later shares that he is one of the two kids with polio, along with his sister Anne. He was quite ill, but recovered as he grew older. He graduated from the University of Oregon in 1970.

In September of 1971, Terry's dad flew around the world. Since Terry had worked at the store since he was 10, his father asked him to be in charge while he was away. Terry responded, "Will you pay me?" The answer was "yes," and Terry ran the store for three months.

In the ensuing years, his siblings did other things, but Terry stuck by his father at the store. He explains his rationale:

"When you figure out what you do well, do it." In 1971, his father was 65 years old and the Eugene St. Vincent de Paul was a small operation, with 17 employees and no safety net. "You worked until you died" was his father's philosophy.

"It seemed to me to be a good thing to help him out so he wouldn't die a pauper," reflects Terry. "There was no career track. It was a dead-end job, and I thought it would be a pity that Dad's work would be lost when he was gone."

I push Terry for his motivation, aside from his father, for sticking with the business. His answer is deadpan. "I needed the money." The reality? He enjoyed making money for St. Vincent de Paul.

Terry is very specific about the date that his father died of a heart attack, as it was the day he became director—April 14, 1984. Only later did I realize that the interview was taking place 30 years to the day after his father's death. Terry reflects:

> *It was 1984, and there was a big recession in Oregon. The most recent recession didn't hold a candle to the '80s. We didn't have the same housing bubble, but in the '80s the state's basic industry collapsed. It just went away. The plywood industry shut down.*

Terry's response to the economic challenges was simple. "Either you go out of business or find a different answer." He wanted to find a way to create jobs and affordable housing. There was no safety net, and he decided he had to find money. "My way to survive was to go to the dump."

Up to this point Terry has been quite reserved, but suddenly he becomes animated and continues:

> *I need to go to other people's dumps. We have two attendants at Portland's transfer sites, five tractors and 200 trailers around the region. We get a couple tons of used candles a month, melt them and sell them back to the craft industry. We sell mattress material and mix it with wax and create fire starters. We take recycled wax, mix it with Crisco, and sell it as skateboard wax. We're putting a new line of jewelry together from old vinyl records... repurposing. We're manufacturing a new line of clothing: UPSMART. We cut out old clothing into different shapes. We turn wide ties into bow ties and cell phone carriers. I have a staff person with an eye for this stuff. We sell 1.2 million used books a year...*

I have to interrupt and ask questions to slow Terry down. He tells me that in 1984 they had 27 employees. Now they have 500 and will have 600 by the end of the year.

Terry continues, "We have more affordable housing than all the St. Vincent de Paul agencies in the country." I respond, "St. Vincent de Paul is doing affordable housing?"

Terry describes how people were being evicted from their homes in the 1980s. In the late '80s he and his board wanted to create housing stock. They started by looking at shelters, as many of the residence hotels were knocked down in the '60s and '70s, and very little transition housing remained for seniors or veterans.

> *Now we are pushing hard into mobile homes. We buy trailer*

parks and help owners purchase new units. It changes the nature of communities. When an affordable housing organization is going out of business, we pick up oddball units that are poor performers—somebody has to.

Terry's organization has housing projects in Mt. Angel, Oak Ridge, Florence, and "everywhere in between." His budget is $25-30 million. He has three goals, the same goals as when he took over as director in 1984: to provide a social safety net, affordable housing, and long-term jobs.

In addition to the job placement efforts that are typical of the thrift industry, Terry wants to create permanent jobs with benefits:

One of our store managers was a poster child for the non-upwardly mobile who had her first child at 13 and her second at 15. The personnel manager started at entry level. An offender charged with manslaughter heads up another division. We need to create more jobs and more businesses and give people a second chance.

St. Vincent de Paul formerly received its tax exempt status from the Catholic Church. With the scandals in the church, the church became concerned about connected organizations due to liability issues. As a result, St. Vincent de Paul now has its 501(c)(3) status separate from the church. "But we still live by Catholic social justice. Our mission requires charity. We do food boxes for people in need and a lot of other services, and all profits go back to community service."

Terry moves into talking about "the next thing." The Robert

Wood Johnson Foundation (RWJ) funded Terry's project, the Cascade Alliance, to develop a mattress recycling project in Bridgeport, Connecticut and a furniture bank in Orlando, Florida. When the grant ended 18 months ago, RWJ came back to Terry and asked him to do the same thing on a larger scale. Seven months later RWJ funded the Cascade Alliance for three years to create waste-based businesses in ten communities around the country.

As Terry puts it:

> *You adapt to the waste stream wherever it is. We are such a wealthy country, and we throw away so much. This is the quintessential win-win. I told the Foundation that if we make this work, we create a trade group. The Cascade Alliance is the hub. If you deal with this group, you will have positive community benefit.*

The three-year project is just beginning in April 2014, 30 years after Terry's dad passed away. Before communities can become affiliates, they must have Terry's approval. But affiliates maintain local control. Terry supports a unique business model:

> *Community and economic development work best when done by the local community. Corporations have no roots any more. The limited liability company (LLC) is a magnificent tool but has lost its soul. If you take the model of the LLC and blend it with a nonprofit and focus on economic development, you create a different tool. Local nonprofits are needed in our communities, with local boards and local missions. The model where people are drawn by money is a shallow model. You're just looking for ways to fill some*

empty spot in your soul.

It is clear by the end of the interview that the source of Terry's inspiration comes not from personal ambition, but from a deeper place. He becomes philosophical:

> *I can't imagine living in a world where the only purpose in life is to feed yourself. If it's all about us, I've chosen the wrong track. We have a much greater purpose. We are called to use the gifts we have and follow the golden rule—the basis of all religions. All of the traditions have similar principles… stewardship of resources, kindness to others, and a sense of belonging and place.*

As Terry walks me out of his office, he greets several of his employees. His parting words to me are: "The best of life is serving humanity. I have a personal debt to the people who work here. I am proud of the wonderful people I get to work with. Together we make a difference."

The Pragmatic Idealist

"It is important to align public and private dollars with the research, get the right people at the table, and focus on action."

Swati Adarkar
March 2013

Swati Adarkar was the first child of immigrant parents. Her grandparents were prominent scholars and leaders in government and academia in India. Her father came to the US to attain his PhD in engineering from Stanford. He met Swati's mother on a ship leaving India as she was headed to the foreign service in Vienna. She later joined him at Stanford.

Swati's parents retained close ties to India, and the family returned frequently when Swati and her brothers were growing up. Those trips back to India were very difficult for Swati. The poverty she saw gave birth to strong values relative to justice, equity and opportunity. "I became increasingly concerned with addressing poverty and social mobility, the balance between individual responsibility and what we owe to the community."

Swati describes her worldview, which emerged from her early

experiences, as the "intersection of idealism, values, and what can be accomplished. Understanding one's gifts and using them for the greatest impact and good is a guiding principle for me."

She went to UCLA and participated in student government, representing 22,000 students as a member of the academic senate. After school, she worked in the nonprofit sector in Los Angeles, focusing on advocacy around issues affecting low-income people. Although she resonated with the causes she was championing, she became increasingly concerned about the nonprofits with which she was interfacing. She began to get "a sense that we needed more strategy and harder-nosed thinking."

These experiences prepared her well for Harvard's Kennedy School, where she attained her Master of Public Administration in her quest to better understand how to lead public organizations.

After obtaining her MPA, she was involved in the early development of several organizations, including Children Now in California and Children First for Oregon, the Oregon Hunger Relief Task Force, and The Children's Institute in Oregon. Her earlier experience and academic training made her more committed than ever to balancing her passion for the cause with a tough-minded insistence on a clear rationale and plan to get there.

When she joined the Children's Institute, Swati found a board made up of influential and generous people with a deep commitment to changing the trajectory of the lives of at risk children. Swati speaks fondly about her colleagues:

I learned a great deal from several business and philanthropic leaders who focused on action and measurable results. For several years I worked with Dick Alexander on a weekly basis. Dick's goal was to give every eligible child access to Head Start. What I think we found in each other was an unusual partnership of two people with very different politics, leadership styles and backgrounds who were able to achieve far greater results by working together. My most important job in the early years of the organization was to support business leaders like Dick to carry the message.

Swati's goal with the Children's Institute has been "to create an intellectually rigorous culture and an interdisciplinary team better able to address the barriers to child and family well-being."

The Institute's success has certainly added the weight of credibility to this approach. Through legislative lobbying, the Institute played a key role in securing an additional $39 million to expand Oregon's Head Start Pre-K program, as well as a first-time state grant of $1 million to Early Head Start to serve vulnerable children—prenatal to three years old—and their families.

She is particularly proud of the launch of Early Works, which established demonstration sites in Portland and the tiny southwest Oregon community of Yoncalla. Early Works addresses the achievement gap by focusing on strategies to affect school readiness and third grade success. The project is something Swati has always wanted to do and reflects one of the six "Forces for Good" in Leslie Crutchfield and Heather Grant's book—linking policy, practice and advocacy.

Swati Adarkar represents a growing number of young leaders in the nonprofit world whose sense of calling and passion is matched by their commitment to follow research and best practices, track and communicate results, and seek allies from the private sector in advocating for support of their goals. She is firm in her belief that "we should give people who want to do this work the training and education needed to adequately prepare them for tackling the country's and world's most persistent and complicated societal problems." The success of The Children's Institute, under the leadership of Swati Adarkar, gives credence to that belief.

The Traveling Teacher

> "Whenever you teach something, you learn. The exchange between the person who sets out to make a difference and the people whose lives are changed is profound."
>
> Bill Rauch
> December 2014

All The Way is a play written by Robert Schenkkan which chronicles the first 11 months of Lyndon B. Johnson's presidency. I was not surprised when *All The Way* won the Tony Award for Best Play in 2014, and Bryan Cranston won a Tony for his portrayal of LBJ. I had seen the play when it debuted in Ashland in 2012, under the direction of the Oregon Shakespeare Festival's artistic director, Bill Rauch. This impressive production was one of many plays commissioned by the Oregon Shakespeare Festival to dramatize moments of change in American history.

When I heard Robert Schenkkan acknowledge Bill Rauch's role in making the play possible, I decided to interview the man who was making such a difference in American theatre from the small town of Ashland, Oregon.

Bill grew up the oldest of four kids in Red Bank, New Jersey. His parents met in eighth grade and performed together as husband and wife at their high school senior play. Bill's father grew up in a small town in New Jersey and enrolled in the Air Force, where he was a safety engineer. The GI Bill propelled him to college, where he became a "marketing guy," working at IBM, GTE and NEC, and moving every two years. His mother had "a ton of careers" before Bill was born, opening two dress shops and working as a teacher and a flight attendant before she married Bill's father at age 30.

"Moving around so much freed me to get to know people quickly and create a safety net wherever I went," reflects Bill.

As a kid, Bill loved theatre and wanted to be an actor. He worked as an usher and janitor at the Westport County Playhouse, where he would see all the plays over and over.

He attended college at Harvard, where he immediately jumped into acting. Strangely, he felt restless as an actor and took advantage of a rare opportunity to direct a play in the spring of his freshman year. "It was like turning on a light switch. Clearly, I was a director and not an actor."

During his undergraduate career at Harvard, Bill directed an astonishing 26 plays, some in traditional theatre settings and some in roving places all over campus, including his dorm basement and marching down the street.

After college, Bill considered starting a "truck theatre," where you get a group of players in a truck and perform in isolated communities. But he changed his mind, realizing that a one-time shot in a community is not enough.

Bill fondly recalls doing a French farce, involving residents at a mental health institution as the actors. The experience showed him what a difference he could make by engaging a community in the production of a play. It provided some of the inspiration for Bill and Alison Carey to found Cornerstone Theater Company in 1986.

> At the time of Cornerstone's founding, only 2% of people in the US attended professional theatre. I became obsessed with doing theatre for the other 98%. We called it a theater (not theatre) company, because we wanted it to be more American.

One of the first productions for the Cornerstone Theater Company was in North Dakota, the state Bill knew the least about. They visited a town which once had 5,000 residents but had been reduced to almost a ghost town of 190. Main Street was a dirt road. Using actors from the community, they produced *Hamlet* in the oldest vaudeville house in North Dakota.

Early in the process, during the first reading of their adaptation of *Hamlet*, an elderly gentleman dropped by. He questioned whether Hamlet was praying or blaspheming when he said, "Oh, God, God." The gentleman commented, "I am a rancher and also a Sunday School teacher. I don't like the language you are using."

Bill's response was to arrange a sit-down in a cafe with some of the ranchers and their wives and argue about the purpose of theatre. Bill thought, "Should we show a sanitized version of life or life as it really is?"

Cornerstone continued to adapt classic plays to the language of local communities all around the country. They did a Greek tragedy on a Paiute reservation in Nevada, a biracial *Romeo and Juliet* using actors from the racially segregated town of Port Gibson, Mississippi, and a Chekhov play in a coal mining community in West Virginia.

After five years in rural communities, they received a grant to hire people from the places they had visited and did a national tour to revisit those towns. The tour became the subject of a documentary.

In 1992 they moved to Los Angeles to explore urban communities and build bridges across geography, workplace, ethnicity and age.

Later, they had an opportunity to play at the Arena Stage in Washington, DC. "It was ironic, since our primary founding purpose was to get away from big-time theatres. We brought in neighborhood performers from Anacostia to perform Dickens' *A Christmas Carol*."

In 2002, Libby Appel, Artistic Director from Oregon Shakespeare Festival in Ashland, invited Bill to direct *Handler* by Robert Schenkkan. Working with a cast comprising only professional actors was very exciting for Bill. "It was an intense experience, getting back to the artist I was at age 19."

When Libby Appel asked him what he wanted to be doing in

five years, Bill responded, "I'd like to be in your job!"

Almost five years to the day following his conversation with Libby Appel, Bill stepped down from his 20-year career at Cornerstone and accepted the position as artistic director of Oregon Shakespeare Festival.

As Bill began his new position in 2007, he was reflecting on how Shakespeare addressed the paramount issue of his time—who would replace Elizabeth I. Shakespeare did this by writing historical plays about dramatic transfers of power which occurred in England's past. "I envisioned that we could create a body of work that dramatized periods of US history."

He invited Cornerstone Theater cofounder Alison Carey to help him. They commissioned 37 plays whose purpose was to dramatize moments of change in American history. To date, 21 plays have been commissioned and six have been performed, both in Ashland and nationally, including Robert Schenkkan's *All The Way*. This helped explain why Mr. Schenkkan had been so effusive in his praise of Bill Rauch at the Tony Awards.

Rauch's seven years at Oregon Shakespeare Festival have been marked by change. From Bill's perspective, "It is great to be this far into theatre and learning completely new things."

He notes that all the classics that had been done previously in Ashland were American and European. "The first play I directed was *Clay Cart*, a 2,500-year-old Sanskrit classic." He went on to bring classics from Nigeria, Japan, China, and Mexico to the Oregon Shakespeare stage.

The "green show" on the square, which precedes the plays, had traditionally been Renaissance dance and music. Rauch brings in mariachis, hip hop dance and other features, which attract not only out-of-town theatre goers, but also locals, to enjoy the festivities.

Rauch reflects on his career in theatre, "Whenever you teach something, you learn. The exchange between the person who sets out to make a difference and the people whose lives are changed is profound."

To end our interview, Bill returns to the tour where the Cornerstone Theater Company visited the rural communities which they had engaged in theatre productions. He talks specifically about the Port Gibson, Mississippi production, where the company performed *Romeo and Juliet,* using black actors to play the Montagues and white actors to play the Capulets.

"We put ourselves on the map with this production, through the documentary and coverage in The New York Times."

When the company returned to Port Gibson during the tour, Rauch was informed that the town had only done one biracial production after Cornerstone left. Bill was crestfallen. "I felt that we had failed."

But people in the community pulled Bill aside and informed him that Port Gibson had been designated a "Main Street USA" town, honored from among 435 towns for having the most racially diverse Main Street Board in the nation. They proudly credited Cornerstone's *Romeo and Juliet* with forging the interracial relationships that made this possible.

When I ask Bill what his reaction was when he heard this, he responds, "I cried."

Acknowledgements

I cannot begin acknowledging anyone before I extend my deepest heartfelt thanks to **the 34 individuals whose stories are the subject of this book**. Just as they were inspired to enter their various nonprofit careers, I was inspired by them, through the interview process, to write this book.

My mother **Gwen Dickson** was the person who instilled in me a sense of social conscience and desire to contribute to the greater good. She was a pioneer woman in the field of psychology who received her Ph.D. at the University of Minnesota in 1934 and went on to a career in vocational counseling, including work with returning World War II veterans and volunteer selection in the earliest days of the Peace Corps.

During my career, which was primarily spent in higher education fundraising and marketing, several people inspired my interest in nonprofit organizations. International organizational development consultant and close friend **Mark Millemann** stirred my interest in organizational theory and leadership development. **John Keyser**, president of Clackamas Community College, was a significant mentor for fifteen years. His support allowed me to provide strategic planning and leadership development assistance to many nonprofit groups in Clackamas County on a pro bono basis, as a community service from the college.

I approached **Jim White**, executive director of the Nonprofit Association of Oregon, to seek his counsel. Jim gave me some valuable advice—to reach out beyond Portland and the Willamette Valley and cover the entire state of Oregon. Jim felt that this would add diversity to the stories and would capture the uniquely Oregon spirit of community service that is at the heart of nonprofit work here in the state. Jim was also instrumental in introducing me to many people around the state whose stories became part of the book.

I could not have completed this book without the support of my family. I still remember my wife **Kate Dickson** telling me three years into the process that I needed to stop interviewing and start writing! Her love and support over seven years were a priceless gift. My daughters **Mollie Harris** and **Rose Dickson** confronted me as we were doing New Year's Resolutions to bring on 2017. I was waxing eloquently (I thought) about how rich and rewarding an experience the interviews were. Maybe turning them into a book would not be necessary. They would have none of this! Together Mollie and Rose, with the firm backing of their godfather **Daniel Johnson**, urged me to move forward on the book.

Acknowledgements

To turn the project from vision to reality, I needed an editor and a publisher. A talented young writer and close friend **Charles Bolton** agreed to lend his considerable skills as editor.

After researching the publishing process, I determined that I did not want to jump through the hoops that a publishing company would invariably put in front of me. I decided to self publish and was delighted when my gifted artist daughter **Rose Dickson** stepped forward to serve as my book designer. It is her creative eye that gives *On Purpose* its visual appeal.

One of the hardest things for me was coming up with the right book title. *Stories from the Lives of Oregon Nonprofit Leaders* was easy. But what simple theme could tie together these 34 stories? *Changing Lives? Leadership Matters? Called to Lead?* My son-in-law **Maury Harris**, who leads the communication efforts for the Community Foundation for Southwest Washington, suggested the winning title—*On Purpose*.

In order to include someone who could lend perspective gained from his own experience in founding nonprofit organizations in Oregon, I contacted **Duncan Campbell** and asked if he would write the foreword to the book. I wanted his reflections on the stories as they related to his unique experience of growing up in a broken family, starting a successful business and then following his heart into the nonprofit world.

Finally, this book is not simply the product of 34 interviews. I interviewed **over 40 nonprofit leaders whose stories are not included**. I made the difficult decisions on whom to include based less on success or accomplishments and more on their life stories and the sources of their inspiration. Among those not chosen are individuals who have made a huge difference through their work. I extend my gratitude to all the people interviewed, as well as the **many hundreds of nonprofit leaders I did not interview**, who continue to do great things, often outside the public spotlight, changing lives in Oregon.

CPSIA information can be obtained
at www.ICGtesting.com
Printed in the USA
JSHW020101150320
4745JS00004B/12

9 780578 637792